DISCOVERY OF A LEARNING BREAKTHROUGH

A Life in Balance

FRANK BELGAU
as told to ERIC BELGAU

Outskirts Press, Inc.
Denver, Colorado

For more information logon to our website: www.learningbreakthrough.com.

Outskirts Press, Inc.
http://www.outskirtspress.com

ISBN: 978-1-4327-4207-2

Outskirts Press and the "OP" logo are trademarks belonging to Outskirts Press, Inc.

PRINTED IN THE UNITED STATES OF AMERICA

DEDICATION

This book is dedicated:

First, to the parents who took upon themselves the responsibility for their children's success, who sought out solutions and demanded results, and who dedicated themselves to learning, understanding, and consistently applying this program;

Second, to the children whose desire to learn outweighed their limitations, who inspired me to look beyond conventional methods and to experiment, and who willingly went with me on a wild ride of discovery; and

Third, to my family and friends, who studied, added to, challenged, and supported my work, and without whom none of this would have happened.

Dr. Frank Belgau

PREFACE FOR
A LIFE IN BALANCE

This is both a beautiful and a useful book. Most books that are beautiful, like art books or books of poetry, are not practically useful while most books that are useful, like cookbooks or phone books, are not beautiful.

This book is beautiful because it tells true stories of heroism, of boys and girls and men and women persisting against odds and common wisdom to discover new truths and develop strengths the world didn't know they had.

This book is useful because it both gives a lesson in how to be a scientist--a discoverer of truth--and it offers up such truth, a breakthrough in mining the treasures of the mind.

I met Frank Belgau once. It was in 2005, I believe, at a convention. I was immediately struck by his passion for what he had discovered. He was at the stage of a man who is nearing the end of his days who has unearthed truths of major importance, but he had not yet seen these truth gain the wide recognition they deserve.

Since then, Frank has teamed up with Louis Weissman to bring his methodology to a larger audience. I am happy to join in that effort, as I have seen firsthand the extraordinary power of the various physical exercises he developed in improving concentration, memory, reading, verbal fluency, and mental dexterity, as well as confidence.

For years I consulted with a man who developed a program based on the principles to Frank Belgau's. I saw many successes with that program, including seeing it help one of my sons. Sadly, that business model failed, so his program is currently unavailable.

Which makes Learning Breakthrough and Frank Belgau's work all the more important now. It is crucial that the world of education reject the disability model and replace it with a strength--based model, a model that asserts every brain possesses talents. It is up to teachers to work with students to develop those talents. Frank Belgau has fashioned unique and powerful tools to do just that.

As you read his moving story--and the stories of many other inspiring individuals presented in these pages--you will grow, as I did, in excitement and optimism. We have so much more to offer these children than demeaning diagnoses, ineffective tutoring, and medications that don't always work.

And these students have so much more to offer the world, given the chance! When they are recognized as champions-in-the-making, as they indeed are, and when they get practical tools like the ones Learning Breakthrough offers, then they can go from the bottom of the class to the top--as Frank Belgau himself did in fifth grade!

Read this beautiful, useful book and take heart. Use the book. Share the book. Tell teachers, tell other adults and professionals, tell the world that there is a too-well-kept secret that can help kids with so-called learning differences become champions.

And give Frank Belgau, brilliant, brave, dear Frank Belgau a tip of your hat. He has made this world a better place.

Edward Hallowell, M.D

TABLE OF CONTENTS

INTRODUCTION

I came out of the womb and onto a balance board.

We lived in a big, white Colonial-style house with blue shutters, surrounded by saws and sanders. Things there didn't go bump in the night; they went whir. The unfinished basement was transformed into a family room—but in our family, that meant something more like an assembly line than a gathering zone.

There was always work to be done and, by the time I was in middle school, I knew how to use a band saw, how to drill iron, and all the items that went into a Learning Breakthrough Kit. I could screw together a balance board in my sleep.

Some families have traditions like Christmas with the grandparents or Friday night movies with popcorn. Our family's traditions involved silkscreening the grids on the balance boards, cutting stacks of plywood, and convening in the family room to do training. Our Friday nights consisted of my dad explaining the workings of the human brain and the kids performing series of tests and learning activities. A large part of my formative years were spent in a motor home, riding through the night to a lecture the next day and subsisting on an unorthodox diet of corned beef hash, fried tuna with rice, and various other culinary delights, cooked in generous quantities of olive oil over the motor home's propane stove.

My love for music began with Vivaldi's "The Four Seasons," which played in the background my dad's training tapes. My love of literature grew from stories chosen for before-and-after reading tests. My love of carpentry was born the day I realized I could sand the curved edge of a rocker on a belt sander without a guide and get it perfect.

When we weren't on the lecture circuit, I noticed that the parents of the other kids at school were different from mine. They worked 9 to 5 jobs.

They earned regular paychecks. Everybody knew and easily understood what these other parents did: they were doctors, lawyers, mechanics, and accountants. Their lives made sense.

My parents' lives didn't make sense. My mom didn't go to the office. When I got home from school, I invariably found her standing in front of the folding machine, cranking out brochures and singing hymns to herself. Or she was sitting at the sewing machine, making red, green, and yellow beanbags so fast her fingers were as blurry as the bobbin. Or she was typing away, describing some new concept that she and my dad had dreamed up while I was at school. My dad worked in his shop making balance boards, wearing a wool hat, his checkered flannel shirt covered with sawdust. Or he wore a suit, which always had a piece of white string hanging out of the pocket, and he got up in front of people and explained things I didn't understand. Or he took off his suit jacket and loosened his tie and played with the kids my friends and I looked down on with a strange, excited glow in his eyes. When people asked me what my dad did, I told them he was an inventor. The name of his company, Perception Development Research Associates, didn't exactly roll off a six-year-old's tongue.

Back then, the only thing I really understood was that, when you stood on the balance board, you had to stand with your feet equal distance from the center and your toes lined up. I knew that because I had heard it a million times.

By the time I reached my teens, I could describe what my dad did. He was more than just an inventor. He developed and recommended a series of balance stimulation exercises to nurture the underlying structures of human intelligence. Those balance stimulation activities changed the brain by correcting the malfunctioning neural systems that caused children to have learning disabilities. If a child read a passage out of a book, then did one of my dad's activity sequences, and read a different passage of the same degree of difficulty, the child would read faster and have better inflection, reading comprehension, would improve, and the child's eyes would work more efficiently. When I was thirteen, a study was conducted at Fidalgo Elementary School in Anacortes, Washington. The study incorporated my dad's program, in conjunction with the Structure of Intellect training system developed by Dr. Mary Meeker. The study proved that the activities were effective. It even showed a six point per year increase in testable IQ.

By that time I had climbed a few rungs up the corporate ladder at Perception Development Research Associates. I was still actively engaged in manual labor, but I was also a therapist-in-training, able to administer the tests and supervise the activities my parents had designed to children participating in our program. I even had my very first corner office: my bedroom was in the front of the house, in the corner, with a marvelous view of the Olympic Mountains. .

When I rolled my sleeves up, loosened my tie, and hunkered down on the floor with the kids my dad was helping, I finally understood why he'd had that strange, excited glow in his eyes. I knew it was possible, by doing those balance board activities, to create a marked change in a child's abilities. More importantly, I discovered how it felt to actually be the one helping that change to take root. Sometimes, when I was helping my mom or dad work with a child, I would see the light come on in the child's eyes. Understanding! I'd see the world coming into focus for that child and, even though it rarely happened instantaneously, the times that it did left me feeling like I'd seen a miracle.

I would probably have followed in my father's footsteps, getting a relevant degree and continuing his work, had it not been for the imposition on my life of the written word. I became a writer, not by choice or because of a desire to be one, but because there were words that wanted to be written down and they wouldn't give me any peace until I'd written them.

It was after I'd been writing for a while that the light came on for me. I was in my early twenties by that time, and because I'd done my dad's training for all those years growing up, I didn't think I needed it any longer. How much balance stimulation does one brain need?

I'd gone to Hollywood to make it big in the movie business, a process that I expected to take six months. More than a year later, I still wasn't a millionaire. I knew I had to get better if I was going to get anywhere. I needed every edge I could get. I called up my mom and dad, and I ordered a Learning Breakthrough. When it arrived a few days later, I set it up in my hot Van Nuys apartment. I put on one of the tapes and, as that familiar Vivaldi played in the background, I began to do beanbag sequences…while standing with my feet an equal distance from center and my toes lined up.

I have a tendency to overdo things. That first day, I did a full hour of Learning Breakthrough exercises before sitting down for four hours at the computer. If you've never tried it, trust me when I say that standing on a balance board for an hour is a long time. But when I sat down and started writing, I could actually feel a change in the way my mind worked.

Fiction is complex. It has space. It has dimension. It has time. It has a sensual component, an emotional component, and a physical component. It is a reproduction of life, and good writing is far less about words than it is about the author's ability to visualize. That day, after an hour on the balance board, I could see the world I was trying to create far more vividly than ever before. I could hold firmly in my mind what the characters were doing while they were off screen, while summoning the mental and emotional states of the ones on screen with greater clarity. It was a breakthrough.

I still imagine what it must be like for children with severe learning disabilities when the great stone that blocks their mental faculties is suddenly rolled out of the way. If it is, as I imagine it to be, an amplified version of what I experienced that day, it's no wonder their eyes light up when it happens.

I can't honestly say I understand everything that the Learning Breakthrough Program does, but I do know that it works.

And because it works, when my dad sat down to write his story, I sat down with him. I went back to my first corner office, watched the old family movies, silk-screened some balance boards, listened to him talk, and tried to find the right words with which to capture his voice. I wrote from his perspective because a man and his ideas cannot be separated. And although it is a nearly impossible task to render faithfully the full breadth and scope of someone else's life, I believe together we have captured at least the substance of his.

We started work on my dad's story at the beginning of 2007. That year, *Little Miss Sunshine* won the Academy Award for best screenplay, and my own childhood flashed suddenly to mind. "Damn," I thought. "If we'd done it as a movie, I would have had my Oscar."

Chapter 1:

THE EARLY DAYS

Houston, 1960

Houston in the early sixties was, in my mind, the quintessential American city. Like nowhere else, at that time the city was blessed with a sense of possibility. Thirty years earlier, the Great Depression had reminded Americans how fragile an economy could be, which had taught the country to count its blessings in times of plenty. World War II had catalyzed one of the nation's most prosperous periods. During the 1950s, the booming expansion of infrastructure, ideals, and wealth had all contributed to a nationwide sense of possibility.

Then Kennedy infused money and his own unique brand of idealistic fervor into the mix. The space program invited all of us, as a nation, to explore this great new frontier stretched out before us. Where would we go? What would space exploration mean for our future? How could we orbit the earth? Could we land on the moon? How deep into Space could we go? These questions fascinated the great scientific thinkers of that time and, as the American epicenter of the Space Program, Houston attracted scientists from around the nation and throughout the free world into perhaps the most lively and imaginative application of physical science in the history of humankind.

There were places, around NASA's labs and around the University of Houston, where an inquisitive, creative person couldn't go without being drawn into an endless stream of conversations about the possibilities awaiting us in space. Groups of physicists sat at outdoor tables working out vector applications in a gravity-free environment. Free thinkers sat under trees and rambled about alien life and the possibilities of establishing colonies in outer space. It seemed that, everywhere you turned, there were dazzlingly brilliant minds, challenged by what seemed to be impossible tasks. They worked together in a spirit of cooperation and respect, each bringing their own unique talents to form a modern-day round table of genius. Their own technical breakthroughs and escalating competition from the Soviet Union urged them forward. And they made the impossible possible.

Up to that fateful day in 1963, Washington, DC, was Camelot. President Kennedy's charisma and grace inspired a fresh wave of patriotism. There were jobs, and working people knew how to work. There were new industries exploding in Texas, California, and Michigan; and the old industries' products were still the best in the world. This was before Vietnam, before the counterculture movements of the 1960s, before the influx of narcotics, before America lost respect for its leaders. It was the time of "Ask not what your country can do for you," "Give a guy a Coke," and "One small step for a man, one giant leap for Mankind."

It was a time when anything seemed possible.

Teaching Unteachable Children

In the early 1960s, my job had nothing to do with the space program although, as a scientist with a background in aviation, I spent plenty of time hanging around with the people whose jobs did. My job had nothing to do with expanding industries, the culture war with Russia, or the dawn of the computer age. At that time, my job was to teach what were then called "minimally brain-injured" children how to read.

It was an impossible task. The status quo in education at the time was that some kids just wouldn't make it. One principal I knew even recommended having them put their heads down on their desks and covering them with newspapers to keep them out of trouble. He was not an ogre—he was a good principal!

Centrally, the problem was that education had developed good processes to test children, to classify them according to their testable "intelligence" and "ability," but we did not have adequate tools to teach, treat, or train people who had learning disabilities. Neuroscience was in its infancy. The technology for brain mapping and detailed analysis of neurological systems did not yet exist. To put it bluntly, the kids in the learning disabilities classroom were just plain dumb. The broad brush with which society had painted them meant they would stay that way. They'd muddle through somehow, as laborers and hourly workers at the lowest end of the economic scale. Academic advancement wouldn't affect their lives one way or another. They were only at school because there was a law saying everybody between six and sixteen *had* to be at school.

I didn't share that idea.

I used to be one of those children. I could not learn to read when my peers could. I did not succeed in school, and I remembered what it felt like to struggle and try and still fail. But I had overcome those disabilities. I had learned to succeed in school, in the Air Force, and in college. I did not understand, at the time, *how* I had overcome my disabilities, nor did I know *how* to teach these children to overcome theirs, but I knew it was possible. And like those wonderful men with their lab coats and ties down at the NASA labs who burned the midnight oil to conquer the mysteries of physics, I was bound and determined to conquer the mysteries of these children's learning disabilities.

I threw myself into the task full bore, using all the remediation methods I had learned in my training. They didn't work. No matter what I tried, it didn't work. And one day, one of the students pointed it out to me. "Mr. Belgau," he said, "we're doing all these things, but I'm not learning to read." I tried to blame him: maybe if he applied himself more, maybe if they *all* applied themselves more.... I tried to blame their parents. I tried to blame the education system. But it didn't matter who or what I blamed. It was my job, regardless of the obstacles and challenges, to teach these children. In the end, the responsibility rested with me.

Like the scientists at NASA, I ultimately decided to experiment, and the classroom became a laboratory. We would try anything that seemed it might work, and we would all pay attention to the results. When we found something that seemed to work, we'd keep doing it. If something didn't work, we would throw it out and move on to something else. There was no theory in this laboratory, no "what if" scenarios. It was the pragmatic environment possible, focused on nothing other than clear, observable results. And it was exciting. The spirit of the time made any kind of crusade seem noble.

As you can probably imagine, we tried a lot of ideas that didn't go anywhere. I spent my days working with the children and my nights reading mountains of literature, some of it clear and scientific and based in hard evidence, some of it wildly theoretical and imaginative. I borrowed insights and inspirations from both. I devised method after method. And finally, one day, we had a breakthrough.

We had been engaged in an activity that would seem completely unrelated to learning: swinging a pendulum ball hung from the ceiling and controlling its trajectory through space. As we always did whenever we tried something new that we hoped would help the children to learn, we did a little reading aloud before working with the pendulum ball and a little reading aloud after; if we detected a difference in the children's reading ability, we would have hit upon something effective. And on that day, one student's reading after the activity showed a marked, observable change in clarity, speed, and inflection. "Mr. Belgau," he said, "I can read better."

A Breakthrough

It has been more than forty years since that day, during which time I have spent thousands of hours observing and working with children. Always, the criterion for success has been the same: what will create an immediate, observable improvement in reading? Always, I have worked to establish environments in which the children themselves were empowered to create, evolve, and refine the ideas I came up with. Always, we have pursued academic success in the spirit of partnership. And always, the results have been nothing short of profound.

One severely learning-disabled child, who could not read at all in his mid teens, worked with my program, made tremendous strides, and grew up to be a successful attorney. A dear friend was told by an eminent neurologist to take her child home and love him for what the child was and to not expect anything more from him because he would never be able to learn. That child used my program and ended up as the head of the drama department at Texas A&M. A girl who was failing all her subjects in elementary school is now in the process of launching a mutual fund. A young man who did hardly any schoolwork because it was such a struggle for him followed my program for three months and then tested into a magnet school for students extremely gifted in science and math. These examples are not unusual or one-off lucky breaks. Almost anyone, regardless of age, regardless of whether they have a learning disability, will show immediate, observable improvements after ten to fifteen minutes of work with this program.

This book shares my program with you by telling the story of how it evolved. Some of the ideas that I brought into that first classroom, and some of the experiences that had shaped me before then, are relevant: they provide a foundation without which my work would not have proceeded as it did. After it began, it was influenced, assisted, advanced, and shaped by what seems now to be a God-sent parade of wonderful minds and good, talented people who used their lives to add something to the world they lived in. The result of my experience is a system that enhances academic performance and physical efficiency by improving the brain structures that underpin human intelligence and performance.

That system is called the Learning Breakthrough Program.

Chapter 2:

THE SLOW KID IN A FAST FAMILY

I came near the end of a long line of brilliant children, and I was not one of them.

My siblings brought home good grades and wonderful comments from school, and every time my mother ran into one of their teachers, she sure to get an earful about how bright and promising her children were. My father traveled a great deal, and when he returned home from a trip, all the kids lined up to tell him about their latest dazzling academic achievements. They were always exceptional. They were all at the top of the charts.

All except me.

In those days, at the beginning of each school year, every student took an IQ test, and we were seated in our classrooms according to our scores. I sat second to last, right in front of Richie Matthews, who would eventually get in trouble for going into the girls' bathroom and taking all his clothes off.

Even when you're a kid, you're judged by the company you keep, and I was not in good company. I was not like my siblings. I was one of the dumb kids.

And what was worse, I felt dumb. Most of the time, I could think my way through things. If I got a problem in my head and decided to figure it out, I would have no trouble. I could see things in my head and build them. I was good at a lot of things. I never imagined I'd have so much trouble in school.

But the lessons in school made my head spin. I saw them through a mental fuzz, as if I had bad eyesight and was trying to read something I couldn't quite focus on. When the teacher explained a concept, the explanation went in one ear and out the other. Nothing seemed to stick. I was like a bucket with a leak, and it didn't matter how much water the teacher or I tried to pour into my head, it would just drain right back out again. My inability to sort out school came as a shock. And a disappointment. I didn't tell my parents where I had been seated. I was afraid of what they'd think.

Bright, Shining Examples

I idolized my father. He was charismatic and brave and resourceful and brimming with new ideas. He had been one of the leading landowners in Miami-Dade County before the market crashed in 1929, and even losing all his money didn't stop him. He picked himself up and went to work as a mechanic, improving engines and inventing ways to make machines work better, generally amazing anybody who came to him with a problem that needed fixing. He was a full-blooded Norwegian, with light blond hair and a strong face and the big hands of a working man. He was also a masterful mathematician, always learning the latest principles, telling us about them as he put them to work with the machines he repaired or built from scratch.

To me, he was a giant among men, and I desperately wanted his approval.

But any time he came back from one of his trips and it was time for us to line up and tell him about our accomplishments during his absence, I trailed at the end of the line nervously, afraid for my turn to come. Invariably, my academic experience consisted of failing or barely passing grades, of concepts malformed and misunderstood, of bits and pieces of information that didn't match up. I would try to explain whatever I was supposed to be learning, but regardless of how hard I tried, it would come out all wrong.

During the first grade, I should have been learning to read, just like my classmates were doing. Reading was an important part of the Belgau family experience. My father took pride in our brilliance, and my mother, an avid reader, was friends with theater elites in New York City. She had even worked with George Gershwin. Reading was a point of pride among the kids, an important rite of passage. It was more than just a matter of understanding the words we read. We read aloud and our readings had to be dramatic, full of feeling and expression so that whomever was listening to us read would enjoy the experience.

"A story is like a song," my mother would say. "You have to make it sing."

But to me, learning to read was like pushing an immovable object up an endless hill. When I looked at the page, the letters swam around each other. The words changed all by themselves, as if they were trying to escape my comprehension, and I just stared at the page, unable to make out the words, unable to understand or describe what was happening. In school, I paid attention. I worked hard at it. I memorized all the letters and all the sounds, and every time I had a little pocket money, I bought a beginner's comic book so I could try to figure out what the words were by looking at the pictures. I would take the books out into a grove behind the house and sit under a tree, spending hours trying desperately to discern what the words meant. But I could not.

A Secret Revealed

I dreaded the day when my father would ask me to read aloud with the rest of the family. As the first term of first grade neared its end, I did my best to keep the inevitable event at bay. My brothers and sisters had all started learning to read before the beginning of their first year in formal school, but I ducked and avoided questions about my progress, hoping against hope that my parents would just forget about it and let me figure it out in my own way.

But the day came. "You must be reading by now, Frank," my father said when it came my turn to tell about school. I didn't say anything. I knew I couldn't lie, but I hoped if I said nothing he would move on to another question, and I'd be off the hook. He didn't. Instead, he took a beginner's book from the bookshelf and handed it to me. "Let's hear you," he smiled.

I was trapped. The thought suddenly occurred to me to run from the room. Maybe if I ran away and hid, by the time they found me, they would be so worried about me that they would have forgotten about the reading. But my father was looking at me expectantly, waiting for yet another dazzling display of reading from his prodigious progeny. The book hung in the air, suspended, it seemed, as if some invisible, oppressive force was dangling it in front of me.

Reluctantly, I took the book. I also took a deep breath, as if preparing to dive into the deep end of the pool, knowing full well I could not swim. I resolved to read well, this time at least, even if never again, all the while knowing I could fly better than I could read.

And as strong as it was, my resolution to read was not enough. Instead of impressing everybody in the room, as I clearly recalled all my elder brothers and sisters had done, I stuttered and stumbled over every word. Each one was a shape-shifting puzzle that I had to figure out at that very moment, under the glare of the family spotlight. I forgot completely about the meaning of words or the fact that these words had been strung together in a story. I just tried to get the sounds out. And they all came in the wrong order, jumbling and tumbling out of my mouth. It must have sounded like gibberish to my family because, when I looked up, they were all looking at me with an odd expression that was part surprise, part disbelief, part compassion, and part ridicule.

Tears pooled in my eyes. I didn't want them there, and I tried to wipe them away, but more came to replace them, and without even thinking I threw the book down, ran out of the house, and hid in the grove where I'd gone with my comic books. I sat under a tree and cried, not because I was sad but because I was angry. It wasn't fair! My brothers and sisters and parents had all learned how to read so effortlessly. It wasn't my fault it was hard for me. What gave them the right to look at me like that? I hated reading. I made up my mind that there was no point in reading anyway. It was stupid, and only stupid people thought it was important. I would refuse to read. I didn't need books. I could get along fine without them.

It was nearly sunset when my father found me. I was still sitting under that same tree, and I didn't plan on moving any time soon. He sat down on the ground next to me, and he didn't say anything. We just sat like that, in silence, for a long, long time. Then he put his arm around me and pulled me to him. "It's hard for you, isn't it?" he asked. I nodded. I didn't want to talk because I was afraid I'd cry again.

"Can you think?" he asked. It seemed like an odd question and I didn't know how to respond. He tried again."When a question comes into your head, can you come up with an answer to it?" I nodded again. When it was my own question, I could always figure out an answer. I could build things, and I could see what to build and how to build it in my mind. "If anybody tells you you're dumb," he said after another pause, "you just tell me. I'll teach them not to make fun of you."

There, for a moment, I felt safe. I knew he loved me and would protect me, and I also knew that even though I couldn't read or remember what I learned in school, he still knew I could think. Suddenly, instead of rejecting reading, I vowed to conquer the task. I promised myself that I would not only learn to read, I would read more and better than anybody else.

But school continued to be a struggle. Every day I dragged myself to school with my brothers and sisters, and every day I went into class and tried to tread water as the rest of my classmates read. I couldn't figure it out. Whenever I was called on to read aloud, I would stutter and stumble, and the other kids would laugh at me. I couldn't tell my father about it; I knew there was nothing he could do. My classmates and teachers would think I was dumb until I proved I wasn't, and day after day, month after month, year after year went by, and I could not prove it.

Turning the Tables

It wasn't just studying that made my school experience so terrible. Physically, I was a mess. When I ran, my feet would get tangled up and I would fall, and making this happen became one of Richie Matthews' favorite pastimes. I was short for my age. He was tall for his age. Both of us sat at the back of the class, and both of us were considered dumb by our schoolmates. For both of us, this caused no end of anger, frustration, sadness, and rage. At least Richie had me to take it out on.

In the 1930s, schoolyards weren't nearly as well monitored as they are now. Bullies had far more freedom to impose their reigns of terror. Richie relished his. He would hide somewhere—behind a corner of the building or behind a tree or behind a rock—and when I came within range, he would suddenly jump out, all flailing arms and legs, and I would take off running. After a few seconds, my feet would get tangled and trip me up. Down I would go, and Richie would loom over me, laughing. "You can't even run!" he'd taunt, and then he'd fall on me and pummel me, still laughing that sadistic laugh.

It became a daily ordeal. Richie didn't want my lunch money. He didn't want anything from me. He only wanted to feel like he was better than someone, and I made a good target. My older brothers told me I had to learn to defend myself, and at night I would lie in bed imagining myself punching back at Richie Matthews, knocking him down, and kicking him in the belly. I would come up with elaborate tactical maneuvers and plans for getting him good. I would imagine beating him to a pulp in full view of my classmates, and even though it was make-believe, it felt good. It even helped me get out some of my own pent-up rage.

But the next day at school, when Richie Matthews jumped at me from his hiding place, my strategies would go out the window. I'd turn and run, down I'd go, and he'd pounce on me, fists and feet flying, until he'd had his fill.

Eventually, I did come up with a plan, and I have the Holy Bible to thank for that. My mother was fond of telling us about David and Goliath, one of her favorite Biblical stories, and even though I wasn't good at retaining information, she told the story enough that eventually the gist of it sank in. One night, as I tried to devise a workable solution to the problem of Richie Matthews, it dawned on me that I was David and Richie Matthews was Goliath. I took to hiding rocks around the playground at school, so when Richie jumped out at me, I wouldn't have far to run to find the means to end the attack. And the best part was I wouldn't be running away from something—I'd be running toward something: one of my piles of rocks. If I managed to get to a pile without tripping, then I'd turn and let the rocks fly, and if enough of them managed to hit him, Richie would back off.

This plan proved successful enough that Richie and I eventually made peace, and I learned an important lesson. If you can beat a bully, he will become your friend, and then he'll stick up for you when the other kids make fun of you. Richie and I became allies against all the smart kids who laughed at us for being unable to read.

But I was determined to get control of my feet. Sports were almost as important to my family's life as reading, and I knew that as I got older, if I couldn't play ball with my brothers, it would be far worse than the trouble I had with not being able to read. Overcoming my awkwardness became an obsession. I vowed I was not going to trip over my feet for the rest of my life.

At the beginning of the summer between fourth and fifth grades, I determined to spend my time out of school conquering my disobedient limbs. In those days, every boy had a paper route, and my brothers and I got up at five o'clock every morning to go out and deliver papers. After we'd completed our routes and chores, we went to the beach. That summer, while my brothers dove into the ocean or went off to climb coconut trees, I taught myself how to run without falling.

Florida beaches are riddled with fiddler crab holes, and when I ran I aimed my feet to fall on the holes, using them like a tire run at football training camp. I was terrible at it at first, not only missing the holes but losing track of my feet as well, tripping frequently and ending up burrowing my own holes in the beach, sometimes face first. But as the summer wore on, I got better and better and, by the end of the summer, I could run at top speed, hitting every hole I aimed at. I could even spot a hole fifteen feet away, close my eyes, and run to it. Or jump up in the air, turn around, and land on the hole.

When I got back to school, I discovered that my summer of exercise had had another benefit. I could read.

Somehow, by getting control of my feet, I had organized what was out of sync in my brain, and the words that had swum on the page lined up in nice, neat rows and proclaimed their meaning to me. The school lessons, too, made sense, and I could remember them without difficulty. The leak in my bucket was sealed. The fuzz in my mind had cleared out. I was normal. Actually, I was better than normal. I was smart.

Years later, I learned that the neurological processes responsible for precise control of the body in three-dimensional space have a profound effect on the timing and efficiency of the brain. Then, as a fifth grader, that didn't matter much. What mattered was that when we took the IQ test at the beginning of the school year, I got to walk from second to last to the very front of the class. What mattered was that when it came time for my brothers and sisters and I to line up and tell my father about what we'd learned, I had plenty to talk about, and when I talked his eyes danced the same way they'd always danced for my brothers and sisters.

What mattered was that I could pick up a book and read aloud for the family. I even had a dramatic flair.

Chapter 3:

UNSEEN MAGIC

I cleaned the chalkboards after school for Mr. Royer.

For as long as I could remember, I'd had in my mind a picture of a scientist, and I wanted more than anything to be one. I figured I'd be a pilot first. My father had flown a pontoon plane in Tampa Bay in the early days of flight, and when World War II began, the courage of military airmen captured the imagination of almost every boy in the country. When I was old enough, I'd go off to war, too, become a flying ace, return home a national hero, and then turn my attention to science. It was a simple plan.

The scientist of my childhood imagination was a romanticized image. Scientists were handsome men, a little rough around the edges, disheveled because their minds were on far more important things than mundane matters like shaving regularly or getting haircuts. They were important because they were smart, and when they walked down the street with their coats buttoned crooked and their wild eyes flashing, they left behind them a wake of looks and awe-tinged whispers of "he's a *scientist*." They were the magicians of the industrial age. They solved our problems, even the ones we didn't yet know we had. They were, for lack of a better word, cool. For years, I had been looking forward to going to junior high school because, in junior high school, I would get to take science class for the first time.

On that auspicious first day of class as a junior high school student, Mr. Royer let me down.

I had been expecting the handsome genius with his mind on more important things than combing his hair. Instead, at the front of my science class, stood an immaculate man, well past seventy, with wispy waves of white hair and clear blue eyes and a frame so aged it seemed to creak when he walked. Mr. Royer was not my idea of a scientist. Mr. Royer was a different thing altogether. Mr. Royer was an old man.

But this was 1942, and all the young men were off fighting the Germans on one side of the world and the Japanese on the other side. There weren't enough teachers, let alone young men, to go around, and in order to keep the schools open, the school boards had had to hire—gasp—old people.

On that first day, I sat quietly in my seat near the front of the class, with my head down, feeling betrayed. Darn those Japanese. Darn those Germans. I'd been looking forward to taking science class for years, and now, when I'd finally reached the science classroom, instead of having a real scientist as a teacher, I had this old man with white hair who didn't look like he knew anything!

And then Mr. Royer introduced himself.

Mr. Royer had worked closely with Thomas Edison. Mr. Royer had been one of the top scientists in the development of precision measuring instruments. Mr. Royer knew people who we read about in magazines and newspapers. Mr. Royer really *was* one of the magicians of the industrial age. I started to listen more carefully, which was really important, since Mr. Royer spoke very softly.

Leaning on the desk at the front of the room, his pale blue eyes placidly surveying his students, Mr. Royer told us what it was like to work with Thomas Edison. Edison, he said, believed that you should try anything and everything in order to find the answer to a problem and then that you should look at your work to see where you went wrong after you'd failed. Because you would fail. You would fail over and over again before—and here Mr. Royer smiled and his eyes sparkled—the light came on.

He went on, telling us how difficult it is to solve any scientific puzzle and, as he spoke, I began to see myself in Edison's shoes, hunched over a workbench hour after hour, shaving and forming filaments out of every substance I could possibly think of, painstakingly building bulb after bulb, allowing my hope to swell as each experiment neared completion, only to be shattered when the filament failed to illuminate. I also thought of a photograph I had seen of a triumphant Thomas Edison standing in an expensive-looking black suit on the steps of some important-looking building, shaking hands with important-looking people. It was the portrait of a man who, through hard work and genius, had carved out a place in the register of scientific advancement, and as a twelve-year-old boy in my first year of junior high school, I resolved to follow in his footsteps and repeat his successes.

While I was making promises to myself and planning my future in my mind, Mr. Royer took out his pocket watch and let it swing gently from the chain. "You can learn more about physics from watching this pendulum," he said, "than I could teach you in years of school." He told us about how Galileo had been fascinated by pendulums, how he had changed the world's understanding of physics by studying them—and how he had suffered at the hands of the authorities for his revolutionary ideas. All the while, Mr. Royer watched the pendulum. His pale blue eyes moved back and forth. A smile clung to the corners of his mouth, as though by watching his pocket watch swing, he was able to see the secrets of the universe.

And then he gave us a problem to solve. "To what rule is the motion of this pendulum calibrated?" he asked. A few of my classmates offered guesses, but he just smiled and said no. We asked him for the answer, and he replied that we'd never learn anything about science that way. "It isn't about having the right answer," he said. "It's about *looking* for the right answer." He left it at that. His question was the prevailing challenge of junior high school science.

A Quiet Genius

Mr. Royer fascinated me. My own father was a giant in my mind, a careening, dazzling, magnetic man who could do anything he chose to do— and who usually did, whether it was right or wrong. Mr. Royer was different. He was soft-spoken, humble, contemplative, incredibly kind, and yet behind those pale blue eyes, I knew there were whole libraries full of knowledge. That knowledge sometimes made him furious. Sometimes it made him laugh. Sometimes it made him sit quietly, his head tilted slightly to the side, gazing at nothing in particular for what seemed like a long time. Regardless of what he was looking at, it always seemed that Mr. Royer saw more than the ordinary person, more than any other person I'd met. I loved his class. I loved talking to him. I cleaned his chalkboard after school every day so I could have a few minutes with just the two of us, to hear him chuckle or fume about whatever was on his mind.

"What do you want to do, Frank?" he asked me one day.

"I want to fly," I said simply.

"Where do you want to go?" he asked.

"I don't know. All over the place," I said.

"Anything else?"

"I want to be a scientist."

This answer seemed to unlock a hidden brilliance in Mr. Royer. He got up from his chair and helped to wipe the chalk off the chalkboard, perhaps so that his message to me, said in his usual soft voice, would better reach its intended mark. "Whatever you do," he told me, "make sure it makes the world a better place. Leave it better than you found it."

"I will," I said. And I meant it. It seemed to me like the highest compliment anyone in the world could possibly bestow upon me, for someone like Mr. Royer to think that I could do anything that meant something. In that moment, I felt as though I was standing on the steps in front of that building right next to Edison, and he was shaking my hand.

A Lingering Problem

But I still hadn't solved the problem of the calibration of the pendulum. No one in my class had solved it, either. I was in my second year of junior high school by this time, and I felt as though the solution was long overdue. I admired Mr. Royer. He seemed to enjoy talking to me. His class and the bits of conversation we had after school were exhilarating. But he had asked that question on our first day of science class, and every day I came to school without an answer. It seemed as though an unpaid debt hung in the air, right alongside that swinging pocket watch. It was a debt I was determined to pay, and even though the answer was elusive, I spent hours every night thinking about it. I drew diagrams and studied all the scientific papers I could understand. I visualized the pocket watch swinging back and forth, back and forth, back and forth. Every night I went to sleep with the question in my mind.

And then one morning I woke up with the answer.

It came as a shock: the perplexing pendulum suddenly seemed simple, incredibly simple; it swung in time to an orchestra of forces, which were arrayed about it so elegantly it seemed incredible to me that such a perfect, invisible thing could exist. It was early, but I crept out into the hallway, where an old grandfather clock stood. I sat on the floor in front of the clock and watched the pendulum swing. I felt as though I was seeing what Mr. Royer had seen on that first day of science class when he had stared at his watch swinging from his hand while asking us the question. It was a peephole into the machinations of the universe, and on that early morning at age thirteen, the world changed.

It is one thing to understand *that* the world works, that there is gravity, for example, that there are solids, liquids, and gases. But it is quite another thing to see *what* is working, especially when you are young and full of curiosity. When you see *what* is working, the world becomes a magical place. Everything you would normally take for granted (like the swing of a pendulum in a grandfather clock) becomes a miracle. Around everything that does happen is an awareness of the million possible events that did *not* happen. Even the most mundane of static objects comes to life because even its stasis is a miracle in the realm of physics.

At thirteen, I didn't just think that I knew the answer. I knew that I understood the answer. I could visualize the relationship of forces that controlled the swinging pendulum. I could see the unseen magic of the universe.

Normally, I walked to school with my brothers and sisters, but that morning I ran. I didn't have a class with Mr. Royer until the afternoon, but I wasn't going to wait until class to tell him. I charged into the school, ran down the hall to his classroom, burst through the door, and said, "Mr. Royer! It's the acceleration of gravity!"

He was sitting behind his desk, reading. He looked up at me, those pale blue eyes peering over the tops of his reading glasses. Those, he took off, and he placed them purposefully on the desk. He leaned back in his chair, still looking at me where I stood, out of breath in his doorway, staring back. Tears came to his eyes, and a smile grew on his face, and his voice was very quiet when he said, "You're right, Frank. You got it."

Chapter 4:

THE RIGHT STUFF

Simple Truths

I joined the Air Force in 1948, holding fast to the dream of becoming a pilot. The world was recovering from World War II, the Red Scare was beginning, and military service was still seen as a civic obligation for able-bodied men. Moreover, the mystique of the military aviator had never been greater: Flyboys walked around the base with a special swagger, their bomber jackets and neatly pressed uniforms a badge of honor and dignity second to none. I looked forward to joining their ranks.

I was able to test out of my high school graduation requirements and two years of college equivalency. I would still have to complete a degree and become an officer in order to become a pilot but, in the interim, I tested high enough on the achievement exams to be offered my choice of career paths. Mr. Royer's repetition of Edison's quotation, "Never trust a man who can't work with his hands," remained clear in my mind, and I decided that my hands needed to know the inner workings of the aircraft I would eventually fly. I signed up for aircraft mechanics and went off to start at technical school in Illinois.

The technical school offered a course in basic operating principles, and this turned out to be one of the most important classes I ever took. Although the intent of the class was to teach the students the operating principles of aircraft, and I did learn them, I grasped what I thought was a more important lesson: that there are basic operating principles to every process. Behind any application rests a general organizational structure, and in order to make sense out of any system, whether it is mechanical, biological, psychological, or spiritual, one first has to understand that organizational structure.

I was so motivated to do well in Basic Operating Principles that I scored extremely well—well enough, in fact, to be offered a teaching position at the technical school. I will never forget Mr. Trexler telling me I was too young to teach, but I was too well-informed for him not to let me teach. My heart swelled with pride when he offered me the position, and at nineteen years old, I began teaching for the Air Force.

I got a mixed reception from the staff of the school. Some thought I was too young and dismissed me as unqualified before they'd gotten to know me. Others were impressed by my youth and cultivated friendships with me. Among these was George Phillips, a farm boy who had worked on the line in England during World War I, in the early days of military aviation. He took me under his wing, and we spent endless hours outside of class discussing everything from women to wars.

George had an intuitive understanding of mechanics and had honed his mechanical acumen by working on the machinery around his family's farm. He was not a book-learner; he was a man who learned with his hands, and his hands were strong, well-worn, and always marked with grease. He had a philosophy about machines, and about airplanes in particular, that was even more basic than the operating principles I had been hired to teach.

"An airplane is supposed to fly," he told me.

Of course. But he meant something deeper than his statement of the obvious. He meant that there was a purpose to the airplane, that without its purpose it was useless, and that everything about the machine itself, and everything related to working on it or operating it, was meant to contribute to that purpose. He told me stories about the planes he and his mates had worked on during the Great War, planes that came back from missions shot up by machine guns, their delicate structures riddled with bullet holes, and about the long hours they'd put in patching the holes and getting the planes ready to fly again. In a combat situation, the planes were necessary. They had to fly because the pilots had missions to carry out. The missions were important to the war effort. The war effort protected the nation he had sworn to serve. "And look, Frank," he said one night, "they were war planes flying dangerous missions. If one of them was shot down, one of them was shot down. It happened. But if you work on a plane and it goes down because the engine kicks out or because the controls jam—if it goes down because of a mechanical failure—you just killed a guy." That is a perspective I never forgot.

The stories George told me were laced with emotion, as if every bolt he had tightened symbolized a dedication to God and Country. And every story he told deepened that dedication in me. I would walk out along the line in the morning and look at the planes, the metallic glint of their broad wings by the morning mist, and I would feel as though I was surrounded by an immense purpose, symbolized in metal and glass and engineered to protect and preserve the nation. The Basic Operating Principles of aircraft were more than equations and theories of flight: they were the ideas upon which the existence of these airplanes was founded. They were the science that made the purpose possible.

George also had a prejudice against bean counters. To him, they just got in the way, with their nasty habit of keeping track of the cost of every nut and bolt and discounting the importance of what these resources did. "An airplane is supposed to fly," he'd say. "If you have to steal something to make it fly, then for God's sake, you steal it." He also had a prejudice against people who made things look good, as opposed to people who actually made things good. To him, people fell into one of those two categories, with the vast majority falling into the former. That, he said, was the reason why it was always an uphill battle getting things to work.

I was busy studying and teaching the Basic Operating Principles of Aircraft at the technical school. During breaks and after work, I was also learning the basic operating principles of society from George Phillips, and from my own youthful sense of duty, as it was formed and shaped by the post-war military ethic. What it all boiled down to was a very simple perception of and attitude toward both aircraft and people.

At the top of that value hierarchy was the purpose. The purpose of an airplane is to fly. The purpose of a soldier is to serve. The purpose of a teacher is to teach. Beneath that purpose were the applications (e.g., the airplane's flight and what went into it, the soldier's service and what went into it, the teacher's teaching plan); and beneath the applications were the basic operating principles (what the airplane needed to fly, the soldier to serve, the teacher to teach). This was a simple view of life, which was possible to maintain in the simple society that existed in the United States at that time.

During the period of my military service, I met plenty of people who made things look good instead of actually making them good. I met plenty of people whose self-image and personal advancement were far more important to them than the job they were supposed to do. But I also met people like George who, in their lives, were true reflections of a value system that was very alive in America at the time. Those people guided me. They motivated me. They taught me. And through my relationships with them, I managed to move steadily up the military ladder because I was unabashedly dedicated to making things work and work well.

I was never more proud than on the day when I checked out my bomber jacket and started the process of becoming a flight engineer. I put on the jacket and walked around the base, and I felt like the most important man in the world. For as long as I could remember, I had waited for this day to come. Now it was here. I was going to be a pilot. I saw how people responded to me, Frank Belgau, the newest member of the flyboy club. And boy did I swagger!

Unfortunately, there was a problem. My eyesight was perfectly good, but my left eye turned in a little. For cosmetic reasons, the Air Force wanted pilots' eyes to be perfect: the brass wanted their pilots to look good. As a result, I underwent optical surgery to correct my imperfect eye, and my great pride quickly turned into one of the biggest let-downs of my life. Optical surgery was not a well-developed science at that time. The officer who conducted my exam referred me to a young friend of his to perform the surgery. The young surgeon wasn't as careful as he could or should have been, and he made a mistake. Instead of straightening my eye, he turned it in further and rotated it seventeen degrees. After that, I didn't meet the optical requirements for flying service, let alone the cosmetic ones.

I went back to mechanics, which, at that point, was my only option, and now instead of teaching, I was shipped out to Asia. Initially deployed to Korea, I was lucky to run into a colonel in Japan who I had impressed back at the base in Illinois, and he gave me a better assignment: observing the mechanics at the Philippine Airlines stationed in tropical Manila. The Philippine Airlines ran an overhaul depot for the U.S. Air Force, and that's where the aircraft in military service were brought for repair. There, the mechanics took the airplanes apart, inspected them from nose to tail, fixed anything that wasn't up to specifications, and put them back together again. Part of my job was to fly along with the crews—first, with the Philippine Airlines test crew, then with the Air Force test crew, and finally with the duty crew that flew the airplane back to its base. It was a good job, partly for the mechanical work and partly for the camaraderie I enjoyed with the flyers. And for a Florida kid in the military, there weren't many locations in the world as ideal as Manila.

It would also be a life-changing experience because of one man.

An Honorable Man

Bim Manzano was the head of operations for the Philippine Airlines when I arrived in Manila, the man in charge of keeping the planes in the air and running on time. He was a small man, quiet and deliberate, with a wonderful sense of humor and a gentle but firm way of dealing with people. My first impression of him was that he was a man who deserved respect and got it, but who never asked for it or demanded it. He earned it quietly. I did not know then that he had been earning it for years.

I was lucky. Because I had been so fascinated by basic operating principles, I didn't look at airplanes only in terms of bolts, panels, and screws; I also looked at them in terms of the dynamics of flight. The mechanics at the overhaul depot were, for the most part, good people who performed quality work, but my training afforded me a unique expertise, and by virtue of that special knowledge, I managed to distinguish myself quickly. When the planes arrived and we took them up for an initial test flight, I challenged myself to visualize, from sounds and vibrations, all the working parts of the aircraft and to diagnose the problems before we took the engines apart. Before long I had a high rate of success, and that got Bim's attention.

Although he was the head of operations, Bim was a flyer at heart, and he and I often took the planes up to test them, with him flying and me diagnosing potential problems. Soon, we became friends. Outside of work, we would drink coffee together in the city. Sometimes in the late afternoon, he would call me to take a plane up and chase a sunset, and we would fly out over the South Pacific, experimenting with altitude and direction to get the best view of those spectacular, tropical sunsets. Once, when a volcano began a slow eruption, we flew out to take a look into the crater, still one of the most awe-inspiring views I have ever seen—and probably the most frightening flight I've ever been on.

Through the course of hundreds of flights and thousands of hours in the air, Bim and I became lifelong friends. And right alongside George Phillips back in Illinois and Mr. Royer in my junior high school science classes, Bim became one of my greatest inspirations.

Bim was a colonel in the U.S. Army at age 22, an impressive feat for an American and unheard of for a native Filipino. His war record had been so outstanding that General MacArthur gave him the honor of accepting the surrender of the Japanese forces in the Philippines, and in the surrender, the Japanese Admiral handed Bim a samurai sword as a symbol of defeat. That sword was worth a quarter of a million dollars in 1945. It had been in the Admiral's family for generations, and it was a symbol of the surrender not only of a military force, but of an Admiral's honor. Bim knew this. After the war, despite the value of the sword and despite the personal status of having it in his possession, he returned it to the Admiral's family because it was the honorable thing to do. Most servicemen who had fought in World War II wouldn't have realized this, but Bim knew that by returning the sword, he would restore honor to the Admiral's family. He also knew the value of honor.

Bim was that kind of man, honest and direct, quick to laugh and quick to enjoy the world around him, and built of sturdy, immovable integrity. Many times, he had been called upon to put his life on the line, and every time he had answered the call. He was a man who would stand for what was right, regardless of the consequences. He was also a man who would never talk about it.

Some people never know that men like Bim Manzano exist. There aren't many of them. Once you meet someone like him, though, it leaves an indelible mark. My friendship with Bim defined friendship at the highest level. Watching him fly and manage the operations of the Philippine Airlines defined excellence at the highest level. Learning about his service (mainly from other people) defined honor at the highest level. These definitions became, in my mind, basic operating principles of life.

Lessons Learned

These were the lessons that I took away from the Air Force when I left to pursue teaching. First, that every system has basic operating principles, and that a study of the system must begin and end with an understanding of those principles. Second, there are people who make things look good and people who make things good, and even though you might be in the minority, it's better to make things good. Third, whatever you do, do it with honor, pursue excellence, and dedicate yourself to something greater than personal reward. And fourth: don't fly over a volcano, even if it's a slow eruption.

Chapter 5:

BEGINNING TO TEACH

Something had gotten into my blood when I taught basic operating principles, and after ten years in the Air Force, it was time to pursue it. I decided to become a teacher.

Histories of the 1960s often refer to the great social changes that came about at that time. There are chapters and whole books about the important and courageous way in which Martin Luther King, Jr., and those who marched and believed with him chased equality. There are volumes on the new idealism, spiritual awakening, and resistance to the Vietnam War. There are books, too, on the dramatic social changes that came from flower power, free love, drugs, and rock and roll.

All of this was alive at the time. All of this was happening. The music got faster, the skirts got shorter, and the voices of the young generation got louder. But that wasn't the only revolution happening in America. There were awakenings of all kinds. And I believe that history shortchanges what was actually a dynamic, multifaceted period of change by focusing so heavily on politics.

Because touched only gently by the political change of the time was a much more earth-shattering, vibrant, and idealistic shift in world consciousness.

While the Beatles were singing "Let it Be," the scientific community around the world was doing anything but that. Rapid-fire scientific discoveries redefined much of our picture of the physical universe. Technological breakthroughs successively changed the way we interact with each other and our world. Every machine improved. Hundreds of old scientific theories were replaced. New technologies burned up the paper on drafting tables one day and lit up cities the next. It was an incredible time.

To me, one example puts this level of change into perspective. When I joined the Air Force in 1948, airplanes with cloth wings, and wooden rudders and propellers were still in service. When I left in 1958, Chuck Yeager had broken the sound barrier in a small, orange wedge of an aircraft powered by a jet engine. In 1969, Neil Armstrong walked on the moon. The students who gathered in protest on the lawns of universities got the press, but the lab coat revolution going on in the buildings behind them defined the age at least as much, and maybe more.

That's the 1960s I remember. That's the revolution I joined.

Opening a New Book

I was honorably discharged from the U.S. Air Force in 1958, just in time to begin the spring semester of college. I was eager to get back into the classroom. Luckily, Dr. Reed Lensley, the Registrar at Sam Houston Teachers' College, took the time to evaluate my prior studies, both at Air Force schools and through university night classes. The nation was growing stronger and livelier every year after the hard economic struggles of the 1930s and the devastating early 1940s. Teachers were in demand; teachers' colleges had to prepare them, and fast. So rather than having me jump through hoops, he gave me credit for everything I'd done in the past—even Principles of Guided Missiles, which, not surprisingly, was not part of the standard teachers' curriculum.

Thanks to his careful evaluation and my own commitment to studying, learning, and getting out into the real world, I finished my bachelor's degree quickly. My first job was teaching fifth grade, which lasted for a year and gave me my first taste of life in the classroom. After that year, I moved to Galveston, Texas, just outside of Houston on the Gulf of Mexico. I started teaching, and I attended night classes at Sam Houston State University, where I received my master's degree in education.

But it was the classroom experience that set the course of my life in motion. I taught mathematics and an arts and crafts class. Arts and crafts was not exactly the place someone like me, with a background in science, engineering, and mechanics, would expect to find himself.

Ironically, it was in the arts and crafts class that my life as a scientist really began.

A Practical Approach to Creativity

Importantly, I came into education from a background that was dominated by practicality, which drove me always to look deeper, to find the underlying principles that defined whatever I was trying to understand. I was my father's son and carried his maxims in my mind: problems are made to be solved; challenges are made to be overcome; if something doesn't work, throw it out, and if something does work, explore it. I brought this frame of mind into the classroom.

In one way, this perspective gave me a great advantage as a teacher. The problem I had before me was to get my students to learn, and because I knew that implicit in every problem is its solution, I brought a great deal of energy to the task. My day did not begin with the morning bell and end when classes got out. I worked around the clock, naturally trying to improve every facet of what I was doing so that it would be of greater benefit to the students.

This perspective was not shared by all of my fellow teachers. It kept me at odds throughout my teaching career (and into later life) with the bureaucracy and resistance to change that are hallmarks of the educational establishment. Early on, I was blissfully unaware of that conflict. I thought, with naïve idealism, that the whole purpose of education was to inspire students to learn, that we were all in the same boat pulling together, and that, bound by the nobility of our position and armed with an ever-increasing body of knowledge, we would revolutionize every aspect of education. As a new teacher living on the outskirts of the most exciting city of its time, in the age of supersonic flight, on the verge of the space age, it felt as though anything was possible.

More than forty years later, I still believe it is. Like any idealistic teacher, I had my hopes and ambitions challenged, stifled, and sometimes crushed by the system of which I was now a part. There were many, many times when I lost faith. But by luck or miracle, I found myself consistently in the company of people who were as driven as I was and who constantly inspired me. Some of them were students who challenged my basic assumptions and in whose service I was forced to push myself for better solutions. Some were educators like me, who were devoted to improving the quality of the education we provided, and who kept their focus on that prize and didn't give a damn about the consequences. Some were parents who were willing to go to any lengths to help their own children. Some were fellow scientists in Houston, who shared my curiosity and passion for what worked.

The story of my life as a teacher and therapist, and the story of the evolution of the methods I've developed, is a story of people. Each of them taught me something. Each of them fixed in its appropriate position some small piece of the puzzle. And although when I started teaching I had no intention of doing anything like what I have done since that first year in Galveston, because of these people, my life was guided closer and closer to a series of discoveries that have changed the way I look at human intelligence—and that have changed the lives of thousands of people around the world.

Chapter 6:

EDWARD

The Student is the Teacher

The first of my great unexpected teachers was a student named Edward, whom I met partway through my first quarter as a teacher in Galveston. I was still green, and I still relied heavily on what I had learned from my courses at the Teacher's College.

Edward wasn't even supposed to be in my class. He came to be by a lucky coincidence. Because I was new at the school and I wanted to get to know my fellow teachers, I spent as much time as I could during my first quarter there in the teachers' lounge, meeting the rest of the staff and establishing foundations on which I hoped to build relationships with them. There, when I'd been at the school for two months or so, I met a young woman named Lois, who taught what were called at the time the educable mentally retarded students. I hadn't seen her before and, when I asked her why she was never in the teacher's lounge, she explained that although she only had ten children in her class, she didn't get a break throughout the day because it was so difficult to manage them. In the course of the conversation, she suggested that her students spend a period each day in my arts and crafts class, so that she could have a break and keep her sanity. She looked me in the eyes in such a way that I could not turn her down. So I agreed, and her students came to my class. Edward was one of them.

In the beginning, I treated the students as if they couldn't do much. That was, at that time, society's expectation of mentally retarded children. They, in turn, created havoc in the class and meddled in the other students' projects, proving that they could do plenty, just not what anybody wanted them to do. I quickly understood why Lois had wanted her daily break. My own sanity started to stretch pretty thin and I looked to the other teachers and the administration for advice. My principal was a good principal, and he really was dedicated to education; his suggestion, which was to sit them at the tables, have them put their heads down, and put a newspaper over their heads, is emblematic of the attitudes that educators had toward these children at that time. Of course, I couldn't do that, nor could I keep them under control with any form of discipline.

Finally, I decided to give them projects that would challenge them—and I told them I expected them to do a good job. Sometimes, when you fail in fighting fire with fire, water will do the trick. I sat them down and laid out the projects before them. I explained carefully what they were to do. And I told them I was going to insist that it be done properly. I was diligent in setting up the work, but I did not expect it to have the effect that it did.

To my surprise, they all completed the project. In fact, although some of them did sloppy work, some also did as well as or better than the other "normal" children in the class. Most importantly, from then on, they were engaged in the classroom. They did good work, *really good* work. And it was at this point that Edward began to stand out.

He had cerebral palsy, was legally blind, and had great difficulty talking. But he also had determination and incredible patience, characteristics that were enhanced, rather than diminished, by his disabilities. He was one of those people who is a mixture of great strength and great fragility. As so often happens with such people, I was more aware of the weakness than the strength, and although I liked him and believed in him right from the beginning, I also treated him with kid gloves. His life seemed full of disappointments, and I didn't want him to be disappointed by his experience in my arts and crafts class.

Consequently, I kicked myself when I let him carry a glass bowl he had made, and he dropped it on the floor.

The glass bowl was the product of a project I had invented to replace a part of the curriculum that called for making copper enamel jewelry. Copper was expensive and, in order to economize, I pounded and shaped stainless steel into the shapes of ashtrays and fruit dishes; essentially, I was making molds on which other dishes could be made. Then I covered the shaped stainless steel pieces with the paint that coated the insides of the kilns to keep objects being fired from sticking to the kiln and let the paint dry. I got leftover panes from a glass shop and had the students paint designs on the flat pieces of glass, using the paint we regularly used for copper enameling. Then, after the glass pieces were all painted, we placed the flat pieces of glass on the stainless steel molds and put them in the kiln. When we took the molds out of the kiln, the copper enamel paint had fused into the glass, the glass had sagged down into the mold, and we were left with beautiful ashtrays and fruit bowls.

Edward put a lot of effort into the project, and as a result he made a very beautiful fruit bowl. He was always determined to do things for himself, and when I offered to take his project out of the kiln and put it on the shelf, he would have none of it. It was his bowl, his success, and he would put it on the shelf *himself*. He tottered over and picked up his bowl. But on the way to the shelf, he dropped it, and that beautiful bowl hit the floor and shattered. He didn't react, at least not the way I had expected. He just stood and looked sadly at the pieces for a long time. I thought he would cry or grow angry—something—but he didn't. And after a while, a little smile spread across his face.

He asked me for a flat piece of stainless steel, and further, he asked me to paint it to keep the glass from sticking. I prepared it for him that night, and the next morning he got Lois to let him into my crafts room while I was teaching math. He carefully put all of the pieces of glass on the flat piece of stainless steel, and as soon as I walked into the crafts room, he asked me to put it in the kiln. When it fired, the glass melted and formed little puddles that later hardened into globs with no sharp edges.

He had also brought an old end table from home; I had no idea how he'd managed to get it to school, but there it was. When the glass globs had cooled, he glued them onto the top of the table and filled the spaces between them with grout. Then he took a piece of scrap leather one of the "regular" students had ruined by cutting a hole in the middle of it. Working slowly, Edward cut the leather to fit the tabletop, tooled a design on it, and used it for a border around the outside of the glass center on the top of the table. Throughout the whole process, as Edward told me the next step he planned to take, two thoughts formed in my mind. One was that I was impressed with his creative thinking and with the fact that, when he was faced with a problem, he worked with it instead of just reacting to it. The other was concern that the task would be too much for him. I didn't want him to be disappointed again, but I also knew he would not accept an offer of help or suggestion to do something easier. I looked on anxiously, waiting to see how it would all turn out, but I let him do it by himself.

The Challenge to Succeed

It was not an easy process; it took considerable time, working at it for only an hour or two per day, but day after day he stuck with it. He would get Lois to open my crafts room door for him if I was teaching elsewhere, and day after day when I arrived at the crafts room, I found he was already there and hard at work. He was labeled as an educable mentally retarded child. He was not supposed to be up to this kind of task. And yet, here he was working harder than any of the other students in the class, even the ones who were naturally talented artists with no learning difficulties or physical limitations whatsoever, and he was doing really impressive work. Just watching him work was inspiring, and I photographed the various stages of the project, as much for me as for him. He took the table apart; he cleaned and sanded each part; he put it back together; he stained, sanded, cleaned, and polished it; he glued the glass pieces on top; he cut wood to frame the glass piece center; he grouted between the glass pieces; he tooled an intricate design on the leather; and finally, he glued the tooled leather on as a border. When he was finished, he stood tottering next to the table, as if watching the leather stain dry. And when I looked through the viewfinder to take the final photograph, I was literally astounded. The beautiful bowl that had crashed to the floor and smashed into a hundred pieces was now a table that was even more beautiful.

We entered the piece in a competition and it won first prize. The prize was sent to the school, and our principal presented it to Edward at a school-wide assembly. This was the same principal who had suggested that I have Edward and the other members of Lois's class put their heads down on tables and cover them with newspapers. The school's assembly hall was filled with the students who made fun of kids like Edward and with teachers who didn't want them in their classes because they were so disruptive. Then Edward's name was called, and as he walked with unbearable slowness from his seat in the audience to the stage, the assembly hall erupted in applause. To this day, it is the longest, most genuine, sustained applause that I have ever witnessed.

Prejudices Shattered

This was 1960. In 1963, Martin Luther King, Jr., and thousands of other nonviolent demonstrators would march through the streets of Birmingham, in front of the people who looked down on them, and compel them to admire the courage and dignity innate in every human being. When clumsy little Edward walked up to collect his prize, he had the same effect on the students and teachers in our school. He had endured plenty of insults. He had been the butt of plenty of cruel jokes. He had felt the same sting I'd felt years before when I was called "stupid." And yet he shone with the unabashed dignity of someone who has accomplished something and knows it.

Edward was nothing less than heroic. Through his diligence and persistence, he overcame not only the physiological and physical obstacles that held him back but also the prejudices of his fellow students and his environment. As a result, he was a tremendous inspiration to me, and he left me thinking that I could and should certainly do more than I was doing with what I was given. He also changed my thinking. When the students came into my class for the first time I shared the prejudices of the other teachers. I was a new teacher trying to make friends with my fellow teachers, and that was the only reason I had agreed to have those mentally retarded children in my class. Edward shattered those prejudices. He taught me that a lion can live inside the skin of even a crippled lamb.

My experience with Edward ignited a passion for finding and cultivating those lions, wherever they were hiding, and to find ways of releasing the potential within them.

Chapter 7:

F. E. MCGAHAN

Another Student Becomes the Teacher

Even though I had completed my master's degree, I continued to take education and psychology courses at the University of Houston.

F. E. McGahan taught a course called "Teaching the Minimally Brain-Injured Child" and, as always seems to happen, I met him by accident. I had intended to take a psychology course to expand my understanding of how psychological factors influence learning, but when I went to the school to enroll, I saw the course description of Mr. McGahan's class. It talked about the normal or above-normal IQ child who was unable to learn in the traditional classroom. Lions hiding inside lambs. I was interested.

The instructors were in a big room adjacent to the registration room, and the deal was sealed when I walked over to meet with the professor whose class I had originally intended to take. Some minds are like chisels, sharp and quick and constantly etching new ideas into the tableau of common knowledge. Other minds are like pillows, soft and comfortable on the one hand and suffocating on the other. The psychology professor was of the latter variety, and after a ten-minute conversation with him, not only was I disinterested in his class, but I was struck with the most visceral urge to avoid him. Then I wandered over to where Mr. McGahan was standing, thinking perhaps he and his class would be more promising..

The first question he asked me was what had sparked my interest in the class. When I told him about Edward, he asked if I thought he was genuinely retarded, and I replied that I believed Edward was a genius in the rough. Mr. McGahan looked at me for a long time, long enough to be a little unnerving, and then he said, "You would be surprised by how many children are destroyed by the prognoses of dumb psychologists who have spent only thirty minutes testing them before labeling them and sending them to a class that the child should never be in. Testing should be designed to provide information on how to teach the child. We have a lot to learn—that's what makes education such a fascinating field."

Fascinating. That's what I thought education should be. If you step back and think for just a minute about how much we learn, how much knowledge we store in our minds, how much understanding we accumulate over the course of a lifetime—even how many advertising jingles and TV show theme songs we know by heart—it is nothing short of astounding. The mechanisms of that learning, how it occurs and how to make it better, are fundamentally fascinating. And I can think of nothing as exciting as an environment in which a collection of great minds throws itself into deciphering and understanding the functions that make that miracle possible. Mr. McGahan's class was just that kind of environment.

Every class was filled with good information, and I was pleased to discover that Mr. McGahan seemed to share my obsession with basic operating principles. We studied a variety of concepts from textbooks, but his lectures and the class discussions he facilitated always dove deeper. Mr. McGahan's course met twice a week, at night. During the rest of my waking hours, I was either teaching or preparing for teaching. I still had the children from Lois's class coming to my arts and crafts room one period a day, so I was constantly interacting with exactly the kind of children we were discussing in Mr. McGahan's course. I studied voraciously; I gobbled up all the knowledge I could from the lectures and discussions, and I took the information and methodology I gleaned back to the classroom and applied it to see how the students responded.

Edward had taught me the invaluable lesson that the children we call "disabled" often have great abilities that are simply not tapped or encouraged in the classroom environment. More and more, I began to see that many of these children could learn. They just learned *differently* than a "normal" child. A child who has difficulty reading, for example, can still acquire knowledge, but how is he to acquire the knowledge contained in books if he cannot read the words?

Halfway through the course, Mr. McGahan asked me if I had time after class to have a cup of coffee with him; of course, I accepted. We sat and talked a little about what he had taught that evening and more generally about teaching a minimally brain-injured child. Then he took me over to introduce me to a friend of his who was also an educator, and the conversation continued. I had an idea that maybe there was a way to teach using a multisensory approach instead of traditional methods, and I shared it with them. I told them about Mr. Royer and his experiences with Thomas Edison and how much importance they had placed on using your hands to learn. I also told them about my own experience working on airplanes and how valuable it was to be able to put your hand in a place that was hard to get at and feel and visualize what you were doing. It seemed to me that much of what we teach in school is abstract. You have to create the picture in your mind in order to understand it. I thought that incorporating multiple senses might help to make that information more concrete, and although I couldn't really articulate what I meant, we still discussed the idea for hours.

This was something unique and truly valuable about Mr. McGahan and the people he kept close to him. If an idea was not complete, if it didn't make sense or click right away, that didn't mean it should be thrown out. Instead, it was something to discuss. It was something to investigate. A complete idea can be applied; it has obvious and immediate value, but that does not make the incomplete idea less valuable. An incomplete idea is the ignition switch of creativity. Mr. McGahan and his cadre of educators knew that. They treated every new idea as a seed that must be nurtured and cared for; as it grows, the seed changes form again and again before it blooms. Sometimes, in the process of discussion, a new idea proved fruitless. But as long as it remained interesting, it was worth discussing and exploring. We invested time, energy, and creativity into seeing whether each idea had merit.

Mr. McGahan, his friend, and I continued to discuss ideas over the following weeks, and at one point, they even came to my classroom to observe what I was doing with the students. I felt very important that day, and I hoped they would be impressed with my ability to get disruptive children to sit still and invest themselves in a task that most teachers would consider too difficult for them. I was surprised when they told me that the thing that impressed them the most about my teaching style was that I moved from student to student, looked them directly in the eye, and had a meaningful dialogue with them.

I was even more surprised when, near the end of the semester, Mr. McGahan asked me to come and work with him. His friend was the superintendent of the North Shore Independent School District, and they had a group of fourth-, fifth-, and sixth-grade children who were very bright but had serious reading problems. They didn't know what would work, only that nothing they had already tried was working. I was qualified simply because I did things differently. When I received the invitation, I felt like a tremendous opportunity had been presented to me: to take on a challenge in the company of people who I knew were also devoted to devising new solutions to learning problems. To say I jumped at it would be a tremendous understatement.

Mr. McGahan and I began to work closely together, and my body of knowledge grew by leaps and bounds. He had developed a preschool test based on Arnold Gesell's Study of the Ages and Stages of child development and on his own careful observation of what a child entering the first grade needed to be able to do in order to be successful and learn to read. There were a number of different tests, but he said the most important things that he observed were the child's ability to hop on one foot, skip, and tie his shoes. When he told me that, I was surprised—I thought he would say that the child had to be able to recognize letters or match sounds to symbols. I remember vividly him smiling and reminding me that I was the one who was always rambling on about basic operating principles. Even if a child couldn't recognize and decode words, he said, as long as he was able to do these physical things efficiently, he would be able to learn to read.

A Student's Insight

Over the next few weeks, while I was in the classroom working with my students, I thought constantly about what he had said, and the dots began to connect in my mind. I was still working through the puzzle of a multisensory approach to learning and what he said made me think about body image, specifically as a precursor to learning. It seemed that hopping on one foot provided a picture of balance and rhythm, tying shoelaces provided a picture of eye-hand coordination, and skipping provided a picture of rhythm and cross-lateral coordination. This also got me thinking more basically, and although the idea was only beginning to form, one day I walked into Mr. McGahan's office and said, "I have an insight into a more basic explanation of what this is showing us." He looked up immediately: he could always be counted on to snap to attention when the word "insight" was uttered. I continued, "The three basic structures that Einstein talks about are space, time, and energy. Tying a shoe involves a high level of understanding and organization of three-dimensional space. It involves a complicated sequence in time. It requires energy. Organizing three-dimensional space, time, and energy must be a fundamental component of human intelligence."

And this is why it is so valuable for us to surround ourselves with sharp minds. In only a moment, Mr. McGahan's mind cut out one meaningful sentence from everything I'd said up to that point, focused on it, and saw its value.. "Organizing three-dimensional space, time, and energy has to be a fundamental element in the development of human intelligence." He made me repeat it a couple of times, and then he said, "If you can put flesh on those bones, I think that you will develop something we can use."

I thought about what he had said and then I recalled something Mr. Royer had talked about. According to Mr. Royer, Aristotle believed that the commonality of the senses is the foundation for abstract thought. Aristotle talked about taste, smell, hearing, sight, touch, and movement—the six senses. I could understand that our sense of vision has definite three-dimensional properties, as do movement and hearing. I could understand that the sense of touch, as it relates to one's own body had definite three-dimensional properties. But I could not, for the life of me, grasp an understanding of the mechanism that integrated and made possible the development of a frame of reference that provided a common three-dimensional connection. I could, in a sense, attribute it to movement in three-dimensional space, but I could not visualize how a child could derive this foundational structure. It would take a long time for me to grasp a structure that I could visualize. It would take years of thinking and a lot more information.

Chapter 8

THE NORTH SHORE STUDENTS

Multisensory Reading

Upon my arrival at North Shore Elementary School, I was assigned a class of fourteen children who had been classified by the testing structure as Minimally Brain Injured, but who were by no means unintelligent. They could learn. They could think. They were just terrible readers, and their inability to read made them losers in the academic environment.

When I walked into the classroom for the first time, I felt good about what I was doing. First, I had developed a great deal of respect for Mr. McGahan, and his invitation to work with him had given me a tremendous boost in my self-confidence. Second, I really felt as though I was getting somewhere with my fledgling idea of a multisensory learning system, and I earnestly believed I was going to be able to contribute something to the world of education. These children, bright kids who were minimally brain-injured, composed in my mind the key to making that contribution. By observing them, I was going to discover how to teach the kids who couldn't learn.

Before classes even started, I discovered one reason why these children—and probably many others—had difficulty reading. The most advanced reading material in their classroom was of a second grade level, which was just far too juvenile for fourth-, fifth-, and sixth-grade kids. The stories were completely uninteresting. In fact, I couldn't find anything in the classroom that held any interest whatsoever, and I began to wonder (I still do) how much of the lack of interest and resistance children have to reading comes from the simple fact that what they're given to read when they are young is a waste of time.

In a different classroom, one meant for "normal" children, I got my hands on a fourth-grade reader. It wasn't much better, and story after story failed to keep my interest. Then, when I was in the middle of the first rather good story I had found, I was called away to attend to other things. When I came back and opened the book again, it was a relief. I had that feeling of joy you get when you read a well-written, well-conceived, satisfying story. I decided I would use that story as a teaching tool with my class.

But how do you make reading a multisensory exercise? Even though I had found the reading material, the question of how to turn it into a multisensory mechanism still plagued me. The school year had already started and I was in the midst of teaching my new class by the time the idea finally came to me—in the morning again, just as I was waking up. I realized that reading silently, perhaps, was a visual exercise, but reading aloud was an auditory-visual exercise. Reading aloud while using a finger to follow along in the text was an auditory-visual-motor exercise. I decided to try an experiment.

I got readers for all the kids, and I went through all the books, marking the story every few paragraphs. At the first paragraph, I put a "1" inside a circle about the size of a quarter. A few short paragraphs later, I put a "2" in a circle. I continued with this process throughout the story. Then I handed the readers out to the children and told them to read along silently while I read the story aloud, and to follow along as they read by sliding their finger across and down the page. Every time I got to one of the circled numbers, I paused and made sure they all knew where we were on the page. Then I continued with the reading.

It was the best class day we had had so far in the year. I read the story twice, and both times, the children followed along and paid attention. Some of them had more difficulty keeping their place than others, and some of them grew visibly frustrated, but these were children who lived with constant frustration at school. In comparison, the reading was smooth sailing. And when I finished reading the story and we had a discussion about what we had read, the children were far more engaged than they had been in anything else we had done. Finally, I had them write down what they remembered from the story and hand it in to me.

The papers they wrote were sloppy. On most of them, the handwriting was barely legible. The spelling was atrocious. Only a couple of them remembered what had happened in the story with clarity. I didn't care about the shortcomings: There was *intelligence* in what they wrote. Over the rest of the year, I would watch that intelligence manifest itself more and more clearly.

Student-Directed Teaching

The next morning one of the children asked if we were going to read and follow along again that day. He said he had lost his place a lot the previous day, but he'd really enjoyed the story. I hadn't taken the time to mark the book for reading aloud as part of that day's lesson, but I wanted to do as much of what interested the kids as possible. Their interest, I reasoned, was the main collateral I had for teaching them. So I gave them some unplanned work to do, and I set about quickly marking the books. While I was busy marking the readers, one child started misbehaving and a couple of the others told him to be quiet and get back to work. This was significant. I remembered children just like these at my old job coming into my arts and crafts room and creating chaos.

We soon read the story I had just finished marking and the children followed along. When we finished reading, one of them said that it was not as good a story as the one I had read to them the day before. When I asked questions about the story we had just read, they did not respond nearly as brilliantly as they had to the more interesting story. As a result, I decided that I would try to read with them only those stories that would hold their interest. In trying to find stories that would meet that criterion, I soon developed a great respect for those few authors of children's books who tell a story well—and a healthy disdain for the masses who do not.

Reading aloud became a regular part of our routine and I came up with dozens of other teaching methods, all using various combinations of the senses in order to try to get around the children's various disabilities. Some of my efforts were modestly successful. Some were not. And in determining the difference, my students became my most valuable resource. They were incredibly honest. When something seemed to work, when they seemed to get it, they were quick to see the improvement and tell me about it. When something wasn't working, they were just as quick to point out that I was wasting my time.

In this regard, I was incredibly lucky to be in a North Shore Elementary School classroom. I had been hired to do something different, not really because I had breakthrough ideas but because I was willing to break the mold, and it is important to remember that, at that time, we had no idea how to teach these children. Their most common life path was to grow up on the fringes of school life and to progress through life in manual-labor and minimum-wage jobs while people with less native intelligence went on to professional schools and graduated to well-paying jobs. All I had to work with on that first day of school was a rudimentary collection of possibilities, the determination to overcome the challenge, and the directive to "do something different."

The Teacher Learns

My students taught me how to teach them and, during the first part of the year, I learned from them some of the most valuable lessons a teacher can learn. I learned to reserve praise for the moments when it was really due, not to dole it out liberally, over-affirming bad work in an attempt to make the student feel good. I learned that they were tougher than any of us imagined, and I learned that although most of them hated school, they genuinely wanted to learn.

Most importantly, I learned that the higher I set the bar for them, the higher these students would reach, and this is a lesson any and every teacher can take to the bank. Far too often, we set the bar just below the perceived ability of the children in our charge, and by so doing, whether as parents or as teachers, we rob those children of an important motivation to push themselves toward success. Ironically, we do it because we want them to succeed; we want them to earn praise because we believe it will boost their self-esteem. But just as I am my own worst critic, these children are their own worst critics as well. If their handwriting is sloppy, they can see it. If they struggle with words while reading, they know it. If they forget something, they know they have forgotten it. When we praise them anyway, they know it is false, and it does nothing for their self-esteem except to condition them to an existence of false affirmation. The more I challenged my students, the more they challenged themselves to succeed.

I recognized their self-awareness and desire to learn and I counted it as success. I could see from our discussions and from the little papers they wrote that they were understanding more and more from the stories we read together. I was having them trace letters with their index finger as a spelling exercise and some of them seemed to be having an easier time spelling words correctly.

But at this point I was making a critical mistake: I was trying to get *around* their disabilities instead of tackling those disabilities head-on. It would take another classroom to teach me that lesson.

Chapter 9:

JACK HARRIS

Jousting Mates

I got to know Jack Harris through Mr. McGahan. Through his work as an educator and a professor at the university, Mr. McGahan attracted people with active minds. His social circle included some of the most interesting people I have ever met. Jack was one of them, and what began as a casual conversation in Mr. McGahan's office grew into one of the most intellectually beneficial and personally rewarding relationships of my life.

Jack wore two hats. He was Director of Special Education and an Elementary school Counselor in the LaPorte School District. Either job would have been difficult for just about anybody, partly because he had to invest so much of himself in so many children with great need and partly because he had to work with a number of people who were quite rigid and restricted his efforts to change and evolve the way his school system treated its students with special needs. Somehow, though, Jack managed to excel in both positions and he maintained a straightforward, chin-up attitude that I admired immediately.

Still, like everyone, sometimes Jack needed to vent, and even though I didn't have nearly the responsibility on my shoulders that he had on his, I could relate to his frustrations. We lived near each other, and we took to walking through the neighborhoods or sitting over coffee a couple times a week, talking about big new ideas and grumbling about small, petty minds. I had less to offer to these conversations than he did, but I did make one valuable contribution. I had learned a series of colorful words in the Air Force, which I think helped to express some of Jack's emotion. Friends do what friends can.

In some ways, our approaches to teaching children with learning problems didn't agree. I was much more focused on the physical dimension and specifically on a multisensory approach to learning. Jack put much more weight on tangible measures, such as intelligence tests and practical classroom productivity. We argued back and forth about the merits of a multisensory approach versus a direct learning-oriented approach, and early on I found myself losing all the arguments. It wasn't just that Jack was good at expressing himself, although he was. It was primarily because I had a bunch of ideas without any center. I could talk around what I meant, but nobody—myself included—had any idea what was at the center of it.

Still, Jack engaged in the arguments. Neither of us was trying to win. We both started with an understanding that what was happening in the classroom proved we didn't have the right answer yet. We argued to take advantage of each other's mind and to develop our own ideas. And although our approaches differed, we never lost sight of the fact that we were on the same team. We were both devoted to teaching children like those in my classroom at North Shore how to succeed in academic environments. We both knew the real battle was not with each other, but with an establishment that felt these kids should be warehoused, allowed to skid through the system, and then left to their own devices. We argued to sharpen our swords for that battle.

A New Set of Student Teachers

Gradually, my friendship with Jack Harris evolved from jousting partners to professional advocates. One Saturday evening while we were visiting, Jack told me he wanted me to work with him in LaPorte. I would be doing essentially what I had been doing at North Shore, but my commute would be twenty-five traffic-heavy miles shorter. With Mr. McGahan's blessing, I accepted Jack's offer, and the following school year Jack gave me another classroom full of boys and girls who would go even further in teaching me how to teach them.

When I moved to the LaPorte School District, Jack gave me a great deal of freedom. I did not know then, nor for many years after, how many battles he fought on my behalf or nearly how strong and resolute he really was. He was quiet about those things, which ultimately allowed me to be far more courageous in my experiments than I would have been if I had known everything that was going on. But Jack was one of those great souls who is devoted to what he believes is right, who will work for it when there's work to do and fight for it when something stands in the way. In his own quiet, diplomatic way, he was one of the giants of what happened in Houston over the next few years. Largely because of him, the two years I spent at LaPorte were among the richest of my professional life.

Chapter 10

THE LAPORTE STUDENTS

Pint-Sized Professors

What I did not realize when I accepted my new role at LaPorte was that I would be walking into a classroom populated with pint-sized professors, all with strong minds and even stronger wills, thinly veiled by their disabilities. This was a den of lions—exactly the kind of lions I wanted to find. The students at North Shore Elementary School had taught me to listen carefully to their observations, a lesson that became invaluable in the dynamic environment I entered in LaPorte. With Jack as a constant support, always challenging my ideas, and with these students, what began as an amorphous collection of thoughts and what-ifs gradually evolved into the beginnings of a picture of the brain's biological development over an individual's lifetime. That picture slowly filled in to accommodate the effect of the brain's evolution on learning, and how to tackle learning disabilities head-on instead of trying to teach around them.

In LaPorte, I began by doing what I had done at North Shore, with an important technological improvement. Jack got me a good tape recorder, and he gave me reel after reel of blank tape (which was expensive in 1964), so I could record the stories for my multisensory reading exercises at home and play them in the classroom. This technique gave me greater freedom to move around the room during the exercise and observe the children following along. I'd developed similar multisensory exercises for spelling and arithmetic, which I also started using. And for the first few weeks, I thought I was doing a good job.

My students seemed interested. Like the kids at North Shore, they enjoyed listening to the stories. They seemed to understand them better when they used the multisensory approach than they had using any other approach I'd tried with them. I also shared with them many of the insights I had gleaned from Mr. Royer when I was a boy, which they took to heart. One of the things I tried to communicate to them was the idea that if you come up with a solution for a problem and it doesn't work, you have to look at what you've done wrong to see how to find a better solution. I had in my mind a picture of creating a collaborative, experimental environment in the classroom, one in which we could all have fun trying many different methods in order to find what would help them the most.

In that regard, I succeeded. Perhaps too well.

A Humbling Moment

One day, partway into the first quarter, one of the students raised his hand and said, "Mr. Belgau, what you're doing isn't working. I'm not learning to read." I was surprised by this simple but profound statement. I started to explain how understanding the material was the first step in learning to read and if they would just bear with the program… But I was interrupted by another student, this one in sixth grade: "Mr. Belgau," she said, "I'm going to junior high next year. If I can't read better than I'm reading now, I'm going to be in trouble." I was shocked. And I was embarrassed. I'd thought what I was doing was working, and now my assumptions were being challenged openly in the middle of class. I started to answer this second student, but before I could finish assembling my response, another one chimed in. "My mother says you're certified to teach us to read," he said. "Why isn't what you're doing working?"

That last student saved the day. He was right. I *WAS* certified. That was the magic word. Who did this rabble of children think they were, questioning *ME*, the adult in the room? I was the certified teacher. I knew what I was doing. I had the high ground.

I started to formulate another reply to justify myself, if only to myself. But I never got it out. One of those pesky whispers that sometimes intrudes on our best justifications made itself heard in the back of my mind, telling me that the children were only doing what I had been teaching them to do. They were taking the lesson from Mr. Royer and Thomas Edison and applying it. They were asking me to look at what I was doing wrong to find a better solution.

I recovered my composure as best as I could, and I leveled with them. I explained that we were trying different things. I wanted those things to work, and of course it hurt that they weren't working. But they knew best what was happening inside their minds. I could monitor their work, but not their real, internal reaction to learning. I promised them that we would experiment some more. We would search for something that really would work. I told them I was in the battle right alongside them, and I was. Even though I wasn't one of the students facing a learning disability at that moment, nothing else in life seemed as important as figuring out how to beat that challenge.

At that point, my role in the classroom changed for good. The mistake I had made in my pretty picture of a collaborative environment was the assumption that I was right. With that assumption blown out of the water, the picture truly came into focus. Over the next few weeks, experimenting with the students and having long discussions with Jack, we hit on a measurement that would define my work for the rest of my life. In order for a solution to be acceptable, it had to create an immediate, observable improvement on a student's ability to read aloud.

To some extent, we were already using the tape recorder to record the students reading aloud, but now it became a core part of our routine. That tape recorder was the stick by which we measured everything we did. Whatever we tried, if we didn't hear a difference in any of the recordings, we would throw it out. If we did hear a difference, we would try to figure out why it had succeeded. Needless to say, we tried plenty of experiments over the next few weeks that had to be thrown out. Creating an immediate, observable improvement in a child's reading is easier said than done.

I didn't realize it at the time, but my students had forced me to tackle their disability head on.

As I tried various methods that did not meet the standard of delivering immediate, observable improvement in a child's reading, various thoughts flew through my mind. Up until that point, I had been moving forward and making progress. I had been getting kudos from people who I liked and respected. It had felt good. But now I was stuck, and because there was no core, no central understanding from which I could build a comprehensive structure for what I thought about the multisensory approach to learning, I found myself swimming. I thought about all the books I had read, all the things I had observed, all the work I had studied. I thought about the successes I'd had at North Shore, which seemed increasingly minor. Often, I thought about the statement I'd made to Mr. McGahan that had so impressed him: "Organizing three-dimensional space, time, and energy has to be a fundamental element in the development of human intelligence."

I started generating a mental list of all the observations I had made of the children from Lois's class, the children I'd worked with at North Shore Elementary, and my new class in LaPorte, focusing specifically on the idea of organizing three-dimensional space. One common thread was the way that the children's bodies were organized. Most of them tended to restrict the swinging of their right arm when they walked. For most of them, the right foot pointed out quite a bit more than the left. The germ of an idea began to grow, and I began to study the students in my LaPorte class more carefully. I had them hop on both feet, and I noticed that their right sides responded more slowly than the left. I had them walk in a straight line, heel-to-toe, and I noticed that they had more trouble lining up their right foot than lining up their left foot. Since most of them were right-handed, it would make sense for the right side of their body to be more efficient than the left—and yet, for these children, the opposite seemed to be true.

The Still-Missing Core

One of the basic principles of a two-engine airplane is the synchronicity between the two engine systems that are fixed on either side of the plane. If one engine puts out more thrust than the other, it causes problems in flight. If the disparity is sufficiently severe, it can cause the plane to go out of control and crash. Remembering this principle caused an idea to begin to percolate: was the issue these children were experiencing related to the balance between the two sides of their bodies?

In the mid-1960s, It was not a popular idea to look for learning ability in the body, but the more I observed the children in my classroom, the more the two problems seemed corollary. And why shouldn't they be? The movement of the body through space is defined by brain functions, just as the ability to read and do arithmetic are defined by brain functions. If the knee bone's connected to the thigh bone, wouldn't it make sense that the various departments in the brain are connected, too? I began to wonder: what if an individual's body provides a graphic representation of the inner workings of the brain?

I had a perceptual motor program that I had been using in North Shore

Elementary. It included motor activities developed by Newell Kephart at Purdue University and a few activities from G. N. Getman, who had worked with Arnold Geselle at Yale. Getman had worked with Kephart before he went to Yale University to work with Geselle, and in their partnership and afterwards, Kephart did some important research, which I found tremendously eye-opening. The activities they had developed were truly useful, and now that I was focusing even more on the physical dimension of intelligence, I began to study them in even more depth. But what I had hoped to find didn't seem to be there in the research. What was that *core* of basic operating principles, that central, unifying idea that would provide a foundation for everything I was doing?

I worked diligently, but it was like I was trying to draw a tree without a trunk. It was difficult to explain my ideas to Jack. My students were receptive and always eager to try whatever new activity I brought for them, but none of the activities achieved the standard of results we were looking for. The weeks rolled by, defined by new questions. How is organizing three-dimensional space fundamental to the development of human intelligence? Is the body's movement through space indeed a graphic representation of the workings of the brain? What activity will rehabilitate faulty spatial organization?

The Pendulum Revisited

Then, one morning, I woke up with a solution. The body is made up of a series of pendulums. The arms and legs are pendulums. The head is an inverted pendulum. What I needed to do was to synchronize the movement of these pendulums, to get the body working as a cohesive, synchronous whole. And the natural way to do that seemed to be by having my students interact with a pendulum.

In theory, a pendulum satisfied the criteria of what I was looking for. The period of its swing is dependent only on the length of the string on which the pendulum is hanging, so as long as the length of that string doesn't change, it will swing in perfect rhythm, no matter how hard you hit it. Its motion through space is calibrated to the acceleration of gravity: during the "fall" period of its swing, the force of gravity overcomes the force of inertia, and during the "climb" period, the force of inertia overcomes the force of gravity. Therefore, interacting with a pendulum involves interacting with the three-dimensional world. The pendulum responds perfectly to any force applied to it, creating instant biofeedback. How well are you interacting with the pendulum? Just watch it swing.

I decided to incorporate pendulum activities into the experimental culture of the classroom. I bought some sponge rubber balls, drilled holes in them, and strung strings through the holes. Because I was focused on integrating the two sides of the body, I also made wooden bats out of dowel sticks and painted them with a series of colored bands. I designed the bats so that the children would have to hold them with both hands, one hand at either end of the bat, and use the space between their hands to direct the pendulum ball. This would require that, in every action they performed, they integrated the two sides of their body. By making the two sides of the body work together, I postulated that I could correct some of the physical problems the children were experiencing, and maybe that would be a way to get at their learning difficulties.. I brought the pendulum balls into the classroom over the weekend and hung them from the ceiling; the brightly colored wooden bats sat on my desk, looking rather handsome, I thought. The students were going to have a surprise when they walked in on Monday morning..

To give the proper picture of how this all looked, I have to confess that I am not the most orderly person. I tend to spend much more time thinking about things than organizing them, and as a result, my classroom was not, shall we say, a paragon of neatness. It was chock full of the various apparatuses I had acquired or built for the activities we had done, and because neither my students nor I worried too much about keeping everything in its place, the classroom space was cluttered.

Also, in order to hang the pendulum balls, I had to displace a few of the tiles from the classroom's drop ceiling. So now there were gaps in the ceiling and sponge rubber balls hanging from the grid on strings, as well as the usual assortment of junk that had been gradually filling the place up. It looked more like a circus tent than a classroom.

To the traditional, strait-laced academic mind, the goings-on in my classroom had been getting progressively weirder. Imagine yourself, for a moment, as a teacher in this school. You've been teaching for fifteen years or so, and for all that time, in every classroom along the corridor there has been the same, pleasant scene: students sitting at their desks, doing their work or listening to their teacher explain a lesson. The scholastic environment then was generally thought of as a rather somber place, the academic equivalent of a church maybe, a place where students went to engage themselves in the hallowed practice of learning.

In that environment, the children who could not learn have, historically, been outcasts. Generally speaking, they have been the children who have not done their lessons, have acted out and had to be disciplined, and have behaved contrarily toward their teachers. They have disrupted the quiet, focused environment that should fill a classroom. Not surprisingly, most teachers thought of these students as the ones who had to be kept under control.

Now imagine yourself walking down the hall of your school and glancing into the classroom where these disruptive students are supposed to be trying to learn. Instead of sitting at their desks, they are flopping around on the floor or hopping on both feet or spinning around in circles or banging out rhythms. Instead of sitting them down and trying to get them to focus on a lesson, their teacher is running around encouraging them to *play*. And they seem to be enjoying themselves. From your own experience with these students in your classroom, you think that if they're enjoying themselves, they must be doing something wrong. You would quite rationally look askance at what was happening in that classroom, and although you would tolerate new ideas to a certain limited extent, you would gradually grow a tad suspicious of a new teacher full of big ideas who continuously breaks the mold.

I was blissfully ignorant, and Jack defended me against attacks I never even heard of until years afterward. I brought in the pendulum balls and the bats. I set them up. I had the children work with them. We experimented with different ways to hit the ball, and we invented a whole variety of games. It was an interesting start, but it also had one serious flaw. It was boring.

The Targeted Pendulum

Just hitting the ball over and over again wasn't enough to keep my students interested for very long. I had to make it more fun for them. This was a lucky thought, as it turns out, because in making it more like a game, I put targets out and encouraged them to hit the ball in such a way that it flew over the top of them. Mainly, I just wanted to make the activity more engaging, but in using the targets, I accidentally increased the intensity of the activity. And dramatically. The targets compelled the students to control the movement of the ball much more precisely, which requires extremely complex mental work.

I had all the students work with the pendulum ball for fifteen minutes after we had done our preliminary reading sample. While they were just starting to do the activity, I noticed that most of them had a great deal of trouble controlling the ball's movement through space, but I also noticed that even over one period of exercise, their movements seemed to smooth out a little. They seemed to get more comfortable, and as they did, they seemed to gain more control.

After the activity, the students recorded another reading sample. I was in the middle of setting up the next activity when one of the students came to me with excitement flashing in his eyes. "Come and listen!" he exclaimed. "This one works!" I tried to be professional and objective, but I was as excited as he was. Together, we walked over to the recorder to listen to his reading. When I heard the two samples, though, my professorial calm evaporated. It was there. There was a marked, undeniable change in his reading.

The change was only verifiable in one student's reading, and it was only an improvement, not a fix. The pendulum exercises were certainly not a miracle cure or anything to run out and brag about, but for me, it was an earth-shattering moment. My beaming student had seen a real, observable improvement in his reading after fifteen minutes of an activity. We had found something that met our standard of success. In some profound and important way, we were on the right track.

Chapter 11

JAMES KOETTING

A New Way of Looking at Things

One of the benefits of moving to LaPorte was that Jack Harris had a knack for seeking out people who were leaders in diverse professions and who were also very interested in the learning-disabled children I had in my class. One of these people was Dr. James Koetting, an optometrist on the faculty at the University of Houston. Dr. Koetting had an almost savant-like ability to read. He could consume vast quantities of highly complex, technical material at an unbelievable rate, and he believed that a large part of reading skill was visual. He would get passionate in an instant when he launched into his warmest subject: that too many children could not read efficiently simply because they had binocular visual problems and that, if their visual processes were refined, they would learn more easily. He envisioned visual testing facilities in large trailers that could move from school to school in order to perform extensive screening of the visual skills necessary for optimum efficiency and success in school.

Dr. Koetting's dream was big in both size and scope, but he was not a pie-in-the-sky kind of person. He had thought through his idea carefully, he knew what equipment and procedures were needed, and he had a good tentative design. (Even today, his mobile testing units would provide an invaluable service.) He also shared the passion of F. E. McGahan and Jack Harris for preschool screening and early remediation, and their three-way evening tirades were a sight to behold. The Communist agitators had nothing

61

on these three learned men, and I can still see Dr. Koetting pounding his fist on a table, counter, or any flat surface that was handy, repeating his mantra: "Get children ready to learn. Remove the blocks to efficient learning right off the bat!"

It was Jack who introduced me to Dr. Koetting. One of the ways in which he facilitated connections between people was to prepare them for their meeting by talking each one up to the other, so by the time two strangers sat down at a table together, they felt both honored and eager to meet the other. Before I met Dr. Koetting, I thought of him as a giant, and Jack must have made me look so good to him that he felt the same about me. It always made for a friendly, positive first meeting, and Jack was so careful about who he kept close to him that the people in his circle were all worthy of his praise.

Dr. Koetting brought a new dimension of the puzzle into focus. When we met, one of his many endeavors involved in a research project to determine the effect of reading on the right and left visual fields in English speakers (reading left to right) versus Hebrew speakers (who read right to left). His discussion of the interaction of the two visual fields was fascinating to me, and it drove me to think even more about the profound impact that the *integration* of the two sides of the body has on every aspect of our lives.

I also began to think about vision as one of the central issues that needed to be tackled in order to help my students learn to read better. From Dr. Koetting, I began to learn that there are many, many visual impairments that go far beyond what can be corrected with lenses. Corrective lenses fix visual acuity, but I began to see that acuity was only the tip of the iceberg. It takes some time, for example, to adjust focus from a near point to a point out in the distance, and the less efficient that process is, the more time it takes a child to move his eyes between his piece of note paper and the chalkboard. If the eyes do not move efficiently from point to point on a page, the child will have more difficulty keeping his place while reading.

At that time, many optometrists focused on correcting vision so that an individual could see clearly at 20 feet (in other words, have 20/20 vision). However, this often caused a child's eyes to over-converge (or cross) when she tried to read or write, making academic work more difficult. One of the many basic difficulties most learning-disabled and hyperactive children have is a correctable vision problem, but even many outstanding optometrists and ophthalmologists didn't test for near-point visual problems. It took too much time, and they had a limited amount of time for each patient. Those outside of the optic professions, meanwhile, rarely looked for learning disabilities in the eye, so a tragic number of these simple, correctable problems went unnoticed and untreated.

A Matter of Efficiency

We were using the term "Minimally Brain Injured" to describe the students in my class, but when Jack, Mr. McGahan, Dr. Koetting, and I would sit and talk, we rarely talked about brain injury or retardation. We talked about efficiency. How could we get visual focus to be more efficient? How could we make knowledge acquisition more efficient? How can we increase the efficiency of the classroom environment, and even of our own minds?

The politically correct idea in education and psychology at that time was that intelligence was fixed, that we were somehow born with a specific level of intelligence that we would have for the rest of our lives. None of us believed that idea and, although we all came from different backgrounds, although we all had different areas of focus and different ambitions, we shared a faith that the human brain could be made more efficient and that, as it became more efficient, it would become more intelligent. This is common knowledge today. Few people still see intelligence as a static quantity. But then, it flew in the face of common knowledge. It was a radical idea, courageous in some circles and blasphemous in others, and it was an idea that challenged some of the basic precepts of education and psychology.

Chapter 12:

A Glorious Time

In the Best Company

You have to appreciate what an amazing situation I found myself in. I was in my fourth year as a teacher. The first one I'd spent in a regular classroom, teaching normal students without the faintest desire to get involved in what I was doing now. During the second year, learning-disabled children had come to me as an accident, the product of my attempt to be friendly. Now, two years later, I was engaged in the most challenging work I'd ever come across and spending my evenings and weekends talking shop with three of the most inquisitive, intelligent, passionate people I'd ever met.

They had all achieved a level of professional eminence far beyond mine. F. E. McGahan taught at the University of Houston and ran special education for the North Shore School District. Jack Harris ran special education for the LaPorte School District as well as being an elementary school counselor. James Koetting was known to be among the brightest faculty members at the University of Houston's College of Optometry, he was one of the first advocates of contact lenses, and he was usually the one sent to learn about new discoveries in optometry in order to bring the information back to the rest of the faculty. Like Mr. Royer, Jack believed that the best way to live was to sit in awe and wonder and to drink in the knowledge and experience of especially accomplished people, a piece of advice I took to heart. Here, I had three of them to talk to on a regular basis.

65

And I had my classroom, which had turned into a functional laboratory, with my students as active participants in the gradual evolution of therapeutic systems that would help them learn. The more successes we had, the greedier we all got for more success, and the students grew increasingly assertive in their dismissal of ideas that didn't work. I knew that their own reactions were the key to finally breaking through their difficulties, so I encouraged their resistance when it was appropriate. I can't even count the number of times one of my students laughed at me and said, "Mr. Belgau, you sure come up with some crackpot ideas."

But some of those crackpot ideas worked, and gradually a picture began to form of what was really standing in the way of these children's ability to learn. I tried more activities, refining the pendulum ball program, adding beanbag exercises, and spending lots of time developing outdoor activities that would promote the refinement of the students' body image. The ones that had the greatest impact almost all involved the integration of the two sides of the body, and as the right-side suppressions I'd observed at North Shore and again here in LaPorte began to improve, so did the children's academic performance.

One thing plagued me: I knew I was on to something, but I still didn't know what was at the core of it. I could say with some certainty that organizing three-dimensional space really was fundamental to the development of human intelligence—or at least to the abilities derived from intelligence—but I couldn't say *why*. As a result, it was still difficult to explain with any measure of clarity what exactly was causing the improvements I was seeing. I could only point to my measure: the activities that we continued to use were the ones that caused an immediate, observable improvement in a child's ability to read out loud.

Trying Anything

I began to bring some of the programs I was learning about into the classroom, , following Edison's edict to try anything. We used the Doman-Delacato program; we used visualization exercises; and we experimented with rhythm.

The experiments with rhythm gave me another important insight into the workings of the mental process, which were clarified one day when I was trying to get a student to visualize a simple spelling word. He was having tremendous difficulty with it: with his eyes closed, he just couldn't "see" the word. How could he learn how to spell if he couldn't see the word in his mind?

Using my pen, I tapped out a light, consistent rhythm on the table, and I told him to visualize one syllable on each beat. What I thought was that if he could focus on a smaller parcel of information, maybe he could get it. What I didn't realize was that rhythm has a tremendous organizational effect on the neurological system. The student closed his eyes. He listened to the rhythm. He tried to visualize one syllable per beat. And he got it. Further, after doing this exercise repetitively, he became able to put the syllables together and to see the word. He also noticed, interestingly, that when he visualized he moved his eyes the same way he would to read.

I continued to come up with plenty of new activities of my own. I was also consuming volumes of information and continually bringing other new activities into the classroom. I knew we needed a system for evaluating these activities. The effects of some therapies are a long time coming. Sometimes they are difficult to observe, and it is always difficult with something as "invisible" as mental processing to establish with absolute clarity that *this* activity produces *that* result. Still, that is the kind of correlation I wanted to be able to represent.

Chapter 13

JOURNEY MENSHEW

Support from Another Corner

Journey Menshew was a soft-spoken, strong-willed Air Force major who had been assigned to NASA. Journey was an organizer, he was relentless, and he had the polished resolve of a military man. When testing designated his son as "minimally brain-injured," he threw himself into finding treatments and therapies that would turn the problem around, and with a gentle, patient, take-charge attitude, he became one of the most assertive and effective members in the Houston Association for Minimally Brain-Injured Children, a support groups for parents and families.

The Association regularly brought together speakers and clinicians, and they often sponsored studies and programs in order to increase understanding and awareness of these "brain injuries," what they meant to the children who suffered from them and the families of those children, and what could be done to treat them. It was a diverse group, but because a good number of its members were affluent and because some of them were reasonably influential, the Association had the money, contacts, and faculty to cultivate the science of learning disabilities. Journey took on a facilitative role within the group and his drive for practical, real-world solutions shaped both the Association's policy and the response from the educational community.

When I first met Journey, I had already begun to make good progress in my own classroom, using the pendulum ball activities, beanbag activities, rhythm activities, and a modification of the Dolman-Delacato model called "Basic Body Movements." The parents of the children in my class had seen positive results. They had suggested that the Association bring me out to give a lecture. Journey met with me to extend the invitation.

A few things were immediately apparent about Journey. The first was that he loved his son and was absolutely determined to find solutions for him. The second was that, in his mind, all the pretty theories and elaborate explanations in the world weren't worth a damn unless they delivered real results. The third was that he wasn't going to waste time on bull. He still had an officer's authority and intensity, and those traits, coupled with the passion of a father dedicated to his son, made him a force to be reckoned with. I would not have liked to be the guy who presented Journey with something that didn't work.

Ultimately, The Houston Association for Minimally Brain-Injured Children became a lightning rod for a whole new way of thinking about learning problems. Through them, I got to know men and women from diverse backgrounds—educators, occupational therapists, and university researchers—who, like me, were trying to piece this puzzle together. Interaction with the members and affiliates of the Association also guided me toward one of the most important revelations of my professional career: the role of balance in the process of brain organization, and in the formulation of the mental structures we use to learn.

After I gave my first presentation, the Association offered to fund a summer program in which I would work with a group of the children of Association members, focusing exclusively on the activities I had developed. The participants in the program would undergo comprehensive tests by students from the College of Optometry at the University of Houston at the beginning of the program and again at the end. This was my opportunity to participate in an exhaustive, scientific study of these wild ideas. It would provide the proof I needed to show that these activities worked. It would also provide invaluable insight into what was working and what wasn't, which would help me to refine my work and, hopefully, to get even better results.

There was only one problem. I would be working with a large group of children, doing physical activities exclusively, outside of the inherently structured environment of a school. (Even though the classroom had a culture of experimentation, that culture was controlled somewhat—and in a good way—by the surrounding order of school life.) In order to take advantage of the Association's offer, I had to figure out how in the world I was going to run the program.

In working through this problem, I stumbled onto something wonderful.

To work with a large group of children, I needed help. Because the parents in the Association were so committed to helping their children, I decided to get that help from them. Consequently, I requested that participating children's parents attend as well, and I collected volunteers to substitute for the parents who were unable to come. I created a series of activity stations, so a child would perform one activity for a period of time, then move on to another activity, and so on. I even automated the process of changing activities by recording "Now move to the next activity" at eight-minute intervals on an audio tape that would play while we were working.

I also had the parents participate in the process of observation. These men and women were highly intelligent. They were educated, professional people, many of them working in some field related either to the oil industry or the Space Program. They were doctors, businessmen, mothers, engineers, and scientists, all with a shared commitment to make the program as successful as it could be, and all with an individual passion to help their own children.

In this environment, each parent or volunteer would supervise one station as different children performed the activity. The children would move. The parents would not. I would keep things running smoothly, answer questions, and help with various children and various stations, as needed. Each parent got to observe all the children performing one activity. They also kept track of their own children, as any parent would, so they simultaneously observed all of the children performing one activity and one child (their own) performing all the activities. I observed all the children, one by one, doing all the activities, and I listened eagerly to the feedback provided by both children and parents.

Because I knew the parents and volunteers were competent, the structure left me the freedom to concentrate totally on the child I was observing at any given time. I could allow each child enough time to really analyze what I was seeing, to experiment, and to learn from each one.

The environment and the summer program were a godsend. First, the before and after testing by the College of Optometry showed demonstrable improvements in a wide variety of areas, including both academic performance and vision. I finally had a leg to stand on. Second, the environment gave me a much better understanding of what was happening with the children, and the suggestions of both parents and children, as well as my own observations, enabled me to hone and refine the activities. Third, I began to see more and more clearly that there was something fundamental at work, and I began to suspect that a golden thread existed that would lead us through all the complexity to a simple understanding.

Chapter 14:

NEWELL KEPHART

The Circle Expands

Dr. Kephart was a man ahead of his time. At the very beginning of my work with learning-disabled children, his observations had guided me, and I must have read everything he'd put down on paper, including a book that was seminal at the time: *The Slow Learner in the Classroom.*

When I was working with the Houston Association for Minimally Brain-Injured Children, he was still at Purdue University, running a testing and therapy lab where he and his graduate students experimented with all kinds of innovative treatments for learning disabilities. I had never met him but, in some way, I felt as though we were kindred spirits, chasing the same elusive answers.

Then Journey decided to take his son up to Dr. Kephart's lab for tests, and he invited me to come along. It was a great opportunity for me: my concept of the nature of children's disabilities was growing by leaps and bounds, and when ideas grow quickly, they need good structure or, like fast-growing plants, they get out of control. I needed relationships with more people who were doing work that was similar to mine, and I looked forward to meeting the illustrious Dr. Kephart.

Our visit to Purdue took a week. Dr. Kephart and his students administered an extensive battery of tests while the parents stood by and observed. Then they crafted an individualized program for the parents to carry out at home. After they had defined the regimen, they spent a couple of days with the parents and the child, teaching them how to do each of the activities on the program sheet. Parents also attended an in-depth lecture, which included practical application.

I liked Dr. Kephart immediately. Too often, it seemed that people who worked with children loved to administer tests and then discuss what the tests showed. They loved to diagnose and explain problems, and when it came to solving those problems, they took the easy route of saying that nobody had come up with a solution yet. To them, it was enough to be able to say, "This is what is wrong."

That wasn't enough for me, and it wasn't enough for Dr. Kephart. He saw tests as the beginning of a *process* of activity and discovery, all directed toward solving the problems that had been identified. His students shared his fervor, and during the week I spent with Journey and his son in Indiana, I felt like I'd traveled away from home to come home. Something amazing was happening at Purdue.

It has never been easy to make things happen. One of the great advantages of being the type of person who administers and explains tests, who identifies the problem but does not venture into the difficult realm of trying to solve it, is that you are safe. If the textbooks say learning disabilities can't be changed and you are the person who is responsible for identifying a learning disability, when you tell the parent that the learning disability can't be changed you are simply passing on the advice of experts. Because those experts are vested with authority, and because the tests are specialized and have been given a seal of approval, people will pay a lot of money for them. They will pay a lot of money to be told there isn't a solution. And there is no risk. There is no danger. Nobody looks askance at what you're doing. Nobody criticizes your methods because you're following the standard approach.

People did criticize Dr. Kephart and he continued his work anyway. I respected him for that.

When I first arrived at Purdue, I was surprised to run into Rhonda Wharry, an old friend I had taken classes with at the University of Houston. She had been studying education and child psychology at that time and trying her best to apply what she was learning to her own son, who was very intelligent and still failing in school. We had come together on that common ground, and she had been as convinced as I was that there was a physical component to intelligence. She had looked for courses at the University of Houston where she could pursue this line of thinking, and she had found none. Instead, she'd been told that if she wanted to waste her time, she should go study with a crackpot like Newell Kephart. So she had.

Through Journey and Rhonda, Dr. Kephart already knew a lot about me, and as soon as we had the opportunity for a good conversation, at a dinner on our third night in Indiana, he launched right in, asking me about one of my own crackpot ideas: the Space Walk.

A Place for the Space Walk

Of all the different activities I had tried at that time, the ones that seemed to deliver the best results involved either the pendulum ball or coordinating the two sides of the body. I wanted to create a system of activities that the students could do, not only during class time, but on their own as well, and I developed a game that I called the Space Walk.

The Space Walk consisted of a series of activities performed in real space. A student would begin by hopping on both feet for a distance of a few feet, then on one foot for about the same distance, then on the other foot for about the same distance again. He would hop around in circles. He would hop as far as he could, keeping his feet together. He would walk heel to toe. He would throw an object out in front of him, close his eyes, and try to walk to it. And so on. I was pleased with the Space Walk when I had it designed. There was only one problem: it would take much more space than was available in the classroom.

The answer was obvious. It would have to be painted outside, on the school's paved playground area.

I knew the principal would never approve of me smearing paint all over the concrete outside the school. I also knew the superintendent, who was supportive of my work, would approve. However, if the principal turned me down and I then went over his head to ask the superintendent directly, it would create a sticky political situation. If I approached the superintendent without consulting the principal first, that would create an even stickier political situation. I had only one option.

I waited until the principal went home for the evening. Then I called his house while I knew he would still be in the car, driving home. (Deviousness was simplerbefore the invention of mobile phones.) As expected, his wife told me he wasn't there, and so I left a message, knowing full well that he wouldn't call me back that night. The principal was quite diligent about keeping his workday free of home-related stresses and his home life free of work-related stress. Knowing this, I went to see the superintendent.

"I want to paint something on the playground," I said. "The principal's gone. I called him at home, but he isn't there. I thought I'd ask you to make sure it doesn't violate the district policy."

The superintendent laughed. He knew what I was doing, but he also knew that I was doing it pretty well. "What are you going to paint, Frank?" he asked.

"It's called the Space Walk. It's a series of activities. A bit like a hopscotch game, but a little bigger."

He laughed again. He probably knew that "a little bigger" was an understatement but, for one reason or another, it didn't bother him. "I don't see a problem," he said. "I can't see how that violates district policy."

So I got to work. By the time I went home that night, it was pretty late, but I had finished painting the Space Walk. It was a little bigger than a hopscotch game. It covered most of the sidewalk.

When the principal arrived at school the next morning, all of the kids were jumping, hopping, twisting, and turning all over the sidewalk. He immediately strode into his office, called Jack, and (I was told later) shouted, "Do you know what he's done now?"

I have always taken it as a personal compliment that Jack didn't need to ask who "he" was.

Obviously, Jack caught hell for me, as he did many times, but it was worth it. Painting the Space Walk enabled me to make a series of extremely important observations about the children in my class, and these observations contributed to everything I would do later. As an activity designed to rehabilitate the neurological organization that I now believed laid the foundation for academic ability, it was extremely successful. More importantly, it was an effective diagnostic tool.

When I took my students out to the Space Walk and had them move through it, I saw their neurological organization at work. It was there in the inability to keep both feet together when hopping. It was there in the difficulty some children had walking heel to toe. It was there in the way some could turn around in one direction while hopping, but not in the other direction. It was dramatic when they threw an object and tried to walk to it with their eyes closed.

I saw that many of the students partially or completely suppressed their right side. I saw that when they moved, they either did not counterbalance their movements or they counterbalanced them spastically. I saw more than ever that, in many cases, there was a complete lack of communication across the midlines of their bodies. To an outside observer, we might have looked ridiculous, but I stood rooted in place because I saw something beautiful.

I saw that orchestra of forces arrayed around them. I saw them trying to learn to dance.

I told the whole story to Dr. Kephart and, for the rest of the evening, we discussed in great depth each aspect of what I'd witnessed. To this day, it is probably one of the most intense and engaging conversations I have had on the nature of the body's relationship with space, and through that conversation he and I forged the beginning of a bond. His ideas had been deemed crazy by plenty of well-respected people with impeccable credentials, but he got results. Mine had been deemed crazy by many of the same people, but I got results. We were allies, and we knew it very quickly.

Anybody who takes a risk in life should have an ally like Newell Kephart. After our conversation, he asked me to lecture to his graduate students and, of course, I accepted. But on the night we'd scheduled for the talk, there was a blizzard and Purdue was a white-out. The students begged Dr. Kephart to let them stay home, to put the lecture off for another day, but he refused. He got them all out of their nice, warm houses to hear me tell them about the things I had observed.

Chapter 15:

A PARTLY COMPLETED PUZZLE

A Theory Takes Shape

A general concept of what was happening in the brains of the children we were working with started to take form. It was not conclusive. It couldn't be. We didn't know enough—science didn't know enough—to paint a comprehensive and definitive portrait of the human brain. But there were enough of us—F. E. McGahan, James Koetting, Jack Harris, Newell Kephart, the Association parents, and students from various disciplines who gravitated toward the work—and we had enough children in programs— roughly 500 in 1963—that we could begin to say some things with certainty.

One was that the senses were all connected. Koetting, with his razor-sharp focus on vision, noticed that a rhythm like the one I had tapped out to help my students learn to visualize words, helped to bring order to the movements of the eye across a page while reading. I discovered that if I planted a beeper in the pendulum ball and had a child lie under it to track its movement, the child tracked the pendulum ball more smoothly. We found that as we incorporated more senses into an activity, the child's performance of the activity became more fluid—and the results of the activity were more profound. "Sensory integration" became a buzzword of our work.

We could also say with confidence that the senses were wired into the brain with more complexity than we had previously thought.

Developmental optometry had begun to experiment with visual training exercises as auxiliary to, and potentially as a replacement for, glasses. Based on these preliminary inroads, we began to grasp that a great deal of "seeing" is actually visual processing, that the eye is only one apparatus in a complex web of neurological systems. We postulated that the same was true for the other senses and that part of sensory integration involved this vast web of processing that was happening, invisibly, behind the scenes.

From watching students on the Space Walk, I knew that a key component of the most successful activities involved getting the two sides of the body to work together. I read about using balance boards to promote integration across the body's midline, and I began to experiment with my own rudimentary designs. When I incorporated the first balance boards into activities involving the pendulum ball, my success rate skyrocketed. We did not know why, but we quickly understood that balance was an important part of our work.

And we knew that it was vital to work with the energy—often excessive, sometimes immature—of the children we were working with. That energy made them disruptive in classrooms. It made them difficult for their parents to manage. It made many of them nearly impossible to control. But it was also a source of great enthusiasm that, when correctly channeled, could quickly turn into tremendous focus. The learning-disabled child's energy is like a wild Mustang, rebellious and very difficult to guide, but potent and wonderful when it's handled appropriately and headed in the right direction.

Our training environments, as a result, were hard for a lot of educators to understand and accept. We made our activities seem like play, and then we let the children *play*—as long as they played our games. We usually had parents in the mix, moving around, participating in the fun. And more often than not, we acted like children, rolling our sleeves up and getting down on the floor with the kids, playing with them so they would play with us, so that they would give us their energy, so that we could channel it in the direction that would help them most.

We knew we had only begun to put flesh on the bones of a comprehensive theory that would explain the success of what we were doing. But simple as it was, it was an idea we could build on. It was an idea that made sense, given what was known at that time about the anatomy of the brain. Most importantly, it was the beginning of an explanation of therapeutic activities that worked.

Well-intentioned medical professionals, including psychologists, had

80

been misdiagnosing, mislabeling, and misdirecting learning-disabled children for years. We could see the harm they had done in the faces of the children in our classrooms. We could also see an alternative. This, almost as much as anything, lit a fire under us to continue, to enhance, and to expand our work.

One story illustrates the prevailing attitude of a frighteningly large portion of the neuro-scientific community at that time. One of my colleagues got a call one evening from his sister, who was in tears because she had been having headaches, she had gone to a neurologist, and he had recommended a lobotomy. She was terrified of what abilities she might lose. She was terrified, too, of the mortal danger the operation presented. She hated the idea of having a portion of her brain cut out, but that was the recommendation of the neurologist – who was also a neurosurgeon. He had told her that unless she handled the problem as he recommended, the headaches would continue and get progressively worse, undermining her ability to enjoy life.

Those of us who worked in developmental therapy believed lobotomies represented the absolute worst kind of medicine, like a politician wanting to solve the homeless problem in a city by bombing the blighted neighborhoods. Certainly, my colleague was of this opinion, and he jumped in with both feet to try to convince his sister not to get the lobotomy. It wasn't easy because the neurologist had explained that she *needed* to get it, and he was, after all, a neurologist.

Finally, my colleague discovered that she was taking birth control pills, and he begged her to go off the pills for a month before she made her decision, just to see if the headaches would go away. (Headaches are a common side-effect of some medications, including birth control pills.) After two weeks off her birth control, her headaches were gone. She was elated. She didn't need the lobotomy after all. A terrible and completely unnecessary tragedy was averted.

After three weeks off the birth control, she was pregnant.

Today, thinking back, I can't imagine how many unnecessary lobotomies were performed. Or how many people's brains were destroyed by strong cocktails of drugs that, in institutions for the learning disabled, were passed out like candy by medical doctors and psychiatrists. I can't imagine the irreparable harm that was done to people who might have had perfectly good, productive lives. I can't imagine the great cost—not in dollars, but in human dignity, in human contribution, and in human life—to our society by those medieval practices.

My colleagues and I believed strongly in what we were doing. We would probably have been more practical in that faith, however, and we would probably have been more discerning in our presentation and in our interaction with other disciplines had we not also been such fierce opponents of those barbaric practices. But those were the times we lived in. A partial picture, an incomplete puzzle, a best guess at what was really going on inside the brains of the children we were working with had to be good enough. We were fighting for our new ideas. We were also fighting against the inhuman practices of well-respected members of the medical and psychiatric communities.

Chapter 16:

THE UNIVERSITY OF HOUSTON

A nucleus of minds was forming in Houston, and it was an increasingly exciting place to live and work. This always seems to happen when people are committed to solving a puzzle, and as more able, active minds join in an effort, progress begins to occur at an increasingly rapid pace. One person working alone, no matter how capable, can only go so far. That person may have good ideas, but the great benefit of a community of minds is its ability to spot and cut out the bad ones. More vibrant minds were added to that group; more ideas came to the forefront, and more erroneous perceptions fell away. We felt as though we were on the verge of something profound.

At that time, intelligence was still very much seen as a static quantity. You were born with a brain and that brain had a certain amount of intelligence; it was your job to do as much as you could with what you had. But we started to see that intelligence is far more dynamic than had previously been thought. Like any other aspect of health, certain behaviors enhance the neurological efficiency while others detract from it. As that new idea began to take shape, and as we found more activities that seemed to have a positive result, we surged forward with even greater energy and enthusiasm.

The collection of minds was also diverse. At its core were the educators, working directly with children, creating new programs and observing their results. Next to us was an increasingly broad spectrum of therapists— optometrists, psychologists, and medical doctors—whose disciplines touched ours and who contributed their ideas and energy to the work.

Around them were the parents of the children we were working with. Those parents included members of every stratum of society, which contributed an intriguing element to the work. We were all participants in a common search for an elusive solution.

Our group also included members of the scientific community that contributed to NASA's space effort. They were highly educated. They were both practical and theoretical. They were physicists, engineers, and mathematicians. They brought their scientific talents—as well as their determination to understand—into the Perceptual Motor Laboratory with their children and, because their minds were inquisitive, they demanded increasingly complete and in-depth answers from us. On the other end of the spectrum were laborers, truck drivers, longshoremen: thick-armed, large-handed, blue collar, direct people who didn't care a hoot for science and theory and long explanations. Every group of parents we spoke with included both ends, as well as many members in the middle, of that spectrum. We had to be scientifically valid enough to satisfy the laboratory intelligentsia and real-world practical enough to make sense to the working men and women whose children sought our help.

Amazingly, I don't remember a single instance when parents clashed because of their backgrounds. We were all in the same boat. We were trying new things because the old things weren't working. Everybody knew the explanations were incomplete because we were learning about what we were doing while we were doing it. The questions uneducated parents asked simplified our answers, and the questions of the scientific elite caused us to question, to keep working, and to dive deeper into the problem.

From this group, tendrils began to extend out into a larger network of minds. Parents explained to their friends what we were doing with the group, and they brought their friends' questions and ideas back to us. One NASA engineer in particular, a brilliant man who was instrumental in the development of the lunar landing simulator, would have involved conversations with his colleagues, and more than once he called me up after them, alive with an idea or brimming with a realization. He was the one who pointed out that when a child directed the pendulum ball to make it go over a target, he was using the same mathematical principles that the most elite physicists in the world were then using to put satellites into orbit.

The community of therapists, too, expanded the resources available to us. We were talking specifically about learning, with a special emphasis on learning to read, but a host of peripheral improvements came from the type of training we were doing. Some speech pathologists noticed that the children with affected speech, often a corollary to certain learning disabilities, spoke more clearly. Physical therapists noticed a dramatic improvement in body image. Psychologists noticed a decrease in behavioral problems. Optometrists noticed that visual acuity improved temporarily— often as much as 10% after only one fifteen-minute session. Audiologists noticed that the children could hear better, and that they could understand more of what they heard. Isolated members of each professional group took back to their colleagues those improvements specific to their discipline, discussed them, and brought new explanations and new energy to the working groups.

After a while, as word of our work spread, we began to attract a steady stream of observers. Some were cynical; they came to see how they could prove us wrong. Most, though, were genuinely interested in the work. They brought their backgrounds, their energy, and their expertise; they contributed to the evolving body of thought coming out of our experiments; and they went away intrigued, often staying in touch and becoming contributing satellites of the group.

Dr. Chester Pfeiffer

Dr. Chester Pfeiffer was one of these. He was Dean of the College of Optometry at the University of Houston and one of the most intelligent, compassionate, and inquisitive men I have ever known. He visited the summer program sponsored by the Houston Association for Minimally Brain Injured-Children because it was his college that had contributed testing and analysis.

He had had polio as a child and, as a result of that illness, he walked slowly and carefully. But he seemed always to be in motion. His eyes took in everything around him. His mind was always working.

His polio had been so severe that he had been confined to an iron lung, and the doctors had told his mother that he would never recover. That wasn't good enough for her. She had heard of Sister Kenny and her revolutionary therapies, and even though the doctors warned her that these controversial therapies would likely kill her son, she still used them. Thanks to his mother's determination to pursue every possible option, Pfeiffer not only survived but he also recovered far more of his physical ability than most medical doctors thought possible. Because of this experience, he was predisposed towards the experimental, rehabilitation-oriented approach that we were taking in the summer program.

He was also one of those wonderful human beings who knows the value of a compliment. To him, a compliment was a precious thing, and he didn't give them out easily. He was very receptive. He was very curious. He was willing to let you talk and talk and think yourself blue in the face, and he would follow along with you and wait patiently until you were done. He had a wonderful way of contributing insight and of asking pointed, probing questions that would send you running back to the drawing board. He laughed easily and smiled even more easily. But he did not pay a compliment unless you'd earned it.

I was understandably anxious when he came to observe. The way the optometry students had described him and the way he was described by those of my associates who knew him cast a long shadow. He had a reputation for curiosity; he also had a reputation for seeing through bull. I knew what I was doing wasn't bull, but I also knew that not everybody bought into my ideas when they saw them at work. If he didn't buy into the ideas, I would have a hard time getting out from under that shadow.

He observed what I was doing with his patient, trademark kindness. I had continued to use the model I had developed for the summer program, with parents staffing the stations and the children moving from station to station to do different activities. My job as facilitator was to move around, working with individual children, fixing anything that went wrong, and observing what was happening. Dr. Pfeiffer made himself a part of the group. He interacted with parents and children freely, with no trace of the academic elitism that is so rampant among university executives. He listened to me explain myself. He asked intelligent questions.

When the session was over, he was excited. My explanations were incomplete. I knew that, and so did he. But he saw the results. He saw children improving over the course of a single session. And he thought that the setup that I had stumbled on for the summer program provided, in his words, "the ideal environment for the observation of children."

That was the first compliment Dr. Pfeiffer paid me. Not long after, he paid me a much larger one: he invited me to come and work at the University.

A Lab in the Halls of Academia

Dr. Pfeiffer realized that if a school of thought were to evolve, it needed two critical elements. The first was support. It needed the backing of a prestigious university that could acquire funding and lend a level of respectability to the independent work of individual researchers. The second was challenge. The minds engaged in the creation of a new picture of how the brain worked needed the opposition of minds of equal power who were skeptical of the work. Through the university, Dr. Pfeiffer designed an environment that would provide both.

When Dr. Pfeiffer hired me, we both knew I had a tough row to hoe. In addition to bringing perceptual motor research into the university, he was collecting skeptics to challenge it. We would be thorns in each other's sides, the work of one group challenging the precepts of the other, the work of the second group criticizing the vision of the first. There would be very little room for error. Research would have to be meticulous, or else it would be torn apart. And because it took time to gain tenure at the university, for the first years at least, while I would have the opportunity to pursue my work, my job would always be on the line. Failure was not an option, but it was very definitely a constant threat.

The culture of conflict evolved quickly. When I was first hired, I didn't have either an office or a classroom, and I conducted my work in the hallways of the College of Optometry. The professors who were there to criticize were, as luck would have it, also personally meticulous. If you were to walk into any of their offices, you would find neatness and order on every shelf and every flat surface. They did not like clutter. They certainly did not like having the halls of their precious college invaded by an excited newbie who hung pendulum balls from the ceiling, spread balance boards all over the floor, and enthusiastically encouraged the children he worked with to play.

For a period of time, the personal conflict actually superseded the professional one. They would complain about me, and Dr. Pfeiffer would call me into his office and, with a twinkle in his eye, explain the latest litany of complaints and his views of possible solutions. His solutions usually involved keeping the halls more orderly and the volume of the training sessions lower. The correction would never be enough, and the professors on the other side of the fence would try to extend them. These counterattacks would propel into Dr. Pfeiffer's office with my own list of complaints, and he would broker another deal. I suspect he laughed about it on his own time, but at work, there was definitely a war going on. Most deans would have been disconcerted by it, but Dr. Pfeiffer wanted that war. He wanted me to challenge everything, more and more vociferously. And he wanted them to challenge me, more and more strictly.

Professionally, the culture of conflict was arrayed around an important issue in optometry at the time. Developmental optometry, which took a more therapeutic approach to correcting visual problems, had been evolving for some time. Structural optometry, the classical version of the discipline, tended to look askance at the claims and practices of the emerging developmental optometrists. Either they dismissed the training therapies entirely, or they argued that these efforts were not worth the time, energy, and resources to solve with training what could quickly and relatively economically be solved with corrective lenses. Dr. Pfeiffer brought them together, with me as a wild card on the experimental side. He believed that although we would fight tooth and nail, over time, we would also establish common ground. This common ground, in the long run, would benefit the field as a whole.

In time, Dr. Pfeiffer found a home out of the hallways for the Perceptual Motor and Visual Perception Lab, in a big room where I continued my work. This lessened the frequency and ferocity of the direct, personal clashes between me and my colleagues, but the professional animosity remained, and Dr. Pfeiffer continued to encourage confrontation, conflict, and challenge.

I will not go so far as to say I was in heaven there, but I am deeply grateful for my time working for Dr. Pfeiffer. His vision created a vital, passionate, challenging landscape. And it forced me to confront perhaps the greatest single problem in my work.

When I had first brought movement exercises into my classroom, the criteria for success had been that an activity had to yield an immediate, observable improvement in a child's ability to read aloud. That standard has remained in place to this day, and my focus as an observer, researcher, and inventor of activities has always been on passing that test. Thus, while I have developed a series of potent, practical activities that work, it has always been a challenge to explain how or why they work.

And it was frustrating—truly frustrating—to work with children in my lab, to demonstrate that, after a period of training with my program, they would show real improvement in reading speed, comprehension, inflection, visual acuity, spatial awareness, and other perceptual and academic processes, and *still* to be unable to convince my colleagues that my approach had merit. There were times when I couldn't stand it, times when I was so frustrated by the setup at the university that I just wanted to throw in the towel and walk—or run at a dead sprint—away. Far away. During those times, it seemed that I would never be able to convince these rigid academics to take their heads out of their books and actually *look* at what was happening. At least, I would never be able to convince them until they deigned to drop by the lab and see it with their own eyes, and this they could never be bothered to do.

However, in those "rigid academics," Dr. Pfeiffer gave me the gift of a lifetime. The great danger with new ideas is that sometimes they stick too easily, and our naïve first impressions of a thing becomes the accepted explanation. This is great if you happen to be the person who comes up with the idea. You get famous. You write a few books. You win illustrious prizes. You retire to Connecticut and live happily ever after.

However, it is not so great for the idea itself. If it is affirmed and accepted before it can mature, it will always remain a naïve first impression. The life cycle of these ideas traces approximately the same trajectory as the life cycle of a successful child actor: premature acclaim followed by excessive criticism and, ultimately, collapse.

Historically, the greatest thinkers have always run up against tremendous opposition throughout their lives. Galileo was imprisoned as a heretic for his mathematics. Rousseau was ridiculed for his egalitarian idea that the state should provide an education to all children. The best ideas never have an easy time lodging themselves in the hearts and minds of a society, and in fact, more often than not, it seems that these ideas succeed in *spite* of society, rather than because of it.

It is easy to point an accusatory finger at a power structure and claim that society just refuses to change or that those in power don't want to lose their influence to those with new ideas. But history consistently shows us that the strongest, most vehement opposition comes from the most committed people. Galileo was opposed by people who were honestly convinced that his radical mathematics would jeopardize the souls of the people they were trying to guide to God. We can come with all kinds of names for those people, but in reality, they are good. They have integrity. They want the best for themselves, for their discipline, and for the people it affects. They are, in short, the guardians of principle and, in many ways, the backbone of culture.

And the truth is that societies don't just oppose good ideas because they are good ideas. They rightly oppose new ideas because they are untested. By opposing them, they challenge the proponents of those ideas. They send them back to the drawing board again and again to the drawing board. And from the new idea, which in its initial form is invariably naïve and half-baked, the truly great idea begins to take shape. These great ideas are the product of both great minds and great opposition; they would never be as complete, as dynamic, or as far-reaching if they had been readily accepted by everyone they were presented to that very first time.

That is what happened at the University of Houston: I was sent back to the drawing board again and again. My work got results, and I took courage from that fact. But my explanations were never good enough, so I was always looking for more. More understanding. More knowledge. A bigger, better, more comprehensive theoretical framework.

Dr. Pfeiffer kept me working, and he kept the culture of conflict alive. He had a tremendously difficult job, trying to keep people focused on what was good and just for everyone, while still worrying about the reputation of the college and the university, about where to find funds for research and where to allocate them when they were found, and of enabling change while keeping peace with those who opposed that change. It was a job he did with grace, and even in the worst of it, when a child in my lab would invent a new activity and I would take him to the Dean's Office to tell Dr. Pfeiffer about it, he would light up and listen closely while the little boy or girl described his invention, and then he would offer his sincere congratulations.

A Functional, Working Formula

I had adopted for the Perceptual Motor and Visual Perception Lab the same formula I had used in the summer program for the Houston Association for Minimally Brain-Injured Children, which we had renamed the Houston Association for Learning Disabilities.

Within the community of parents of children with learning disabilities, the program had earned a solid reputation, and there was never a shortage of parents wanting to enroll their children. Given that there were more applicants than places in the room, I could make demands, and the one requirement I had was that *both* parents had to accompany their child to the training sessions and participate, as the Association parents had done during the summer program.

Thus, although I was constantly challenged by my colleagues on the structural optometry side, I was constantly encouraged and fed new understanding by the often brilliant men and women who brought their children through the Lab and by the faculty members on the developmental optometry side. I also learned an incredible amount from the children themselves.

I felt then, and over the years this feeling has only grown stronger, that in therapy as much as in education, our first obligation is to care about the people we are trying to help – to care about them, and to get to know them. A therapist who does not know his or her patient is one who is not emotionally invested in that patient's success. Moreover, by learning about those we are committed to help, we learn better *how* to help each of them on an individual basis.

As I got to know the children who came through the lab, as I talked with them and heard their take on what was happening, they helped to explain what was happening in their own heads. They helped to paint a picture of what it was like to think inside the bubble of a learning disability, what happened when they began to break through it, which activities had the most impact, and which ones were least effective.

It had been more than forty years since I had sat in the back of the classroom, classified as a low achiever by the intelligence tests I had taken. I had never forgotten how it felt. The memory of those feelings, the frustration, anger, and self-doubt that had been such a constant part of my early education was always with me, motivating me to do my level best for every child I worked with, driving me to find an efficient course through the learning disability labyrinth.

Even if I hadn't remembered those feelings of being labeled a low achiever, the pictures these children drew for me would have reminded me. They expanded my awareness of what exactly we were up against. When the pressure from my colleagues got to be overwhelming, or on those depressing days when I came in with a new explanation only to have it shot down, those kids kept me going. I knew what they were going through. I knew there was a way through. It was never possible to walk away. What I felt in reaction to the other esteemed professors' criticism was nothing compared to what these children felt when presented with a book to read.

Chapter 17:

BEVERLEY

One day, while my lab group and I were outside observing the children walk, skip, jump in various ways, and walk a line with their eyes closed, I noticed a very attractive woman studying the children with great intensity. Her daughter, an obviously bright young girl who was failing academically, was in the group, but this woman was watching *all* the children. She asked questions that not only showed she had listened and understood what I had told the group, but that she was reaching further in her own mind. Her blue eyes sparkled with a native curiosity, and when she noted the inefficiencies in the children's movements, she was dead on.

As we walked to the door, she was walking behind me, and I overheard one of the fathers in the group thanking her for the questions she had asked and for the observations she had made: they had helped him to understand what was going on. A few minutes later, when the parents took their children to the activity area, I observed the most beautiful, graceful walk that I had ever seen.

I have always been especially observant of people's walks. Even in the Air Force, when I was going to fly with a new pilot for the first time, I always watched the way that he walked; I found it was a predictor of how he would handle the aircraft. If he slouched or didn't swing his arms when he walked, he would fly sloppily; if he walked with synchronicity and swung his arms in matching rhythm, I knew he would be a good pilot. That remained one of the ways that I judged people; a person's character is always evident in his walk, and I am rarely wrong. I was so conscious of how people walked that I could recognize people at a distance by watching them move. After I began to work with children, I found that by observing their walk, I could see the inefficiencies in their brain processing. It was a natural thing for me to do.

This woman's walk was far better than any Air Force pilot's.

Part of my role as leader of the Perceptual Motor and Visual Perception Lab was to give lectures on Wednesday nights. Lecturing weekly to a group whose members came from all different walks of life and all educational backgrounds, I'd learned to constantly read the audience to see if they were understanding what I was saying: I felt most successful when an accomplished CalTech scientist and a truck driver complimented me after the same lecture. I was aware that I was still working out on the fringe, dealing with ideas that hadn't been accepted by the mainstream, so I learned to remain on guard. If someone in the group decided to challenge the thinking caustically, I had to be prepared to respond honestly, but in such a way that it didn't disrupt the group dynamic.

So I was always very conscious of the audience when I lectured. On that Wednesday night, I remember seeing the same attractive young woman, sitting with her body taut, listening with intensity and focus. Most of the people in almost every group understood the broad structure of what I was saying, but the most critical elements were also the most subtle—and she seemed to hone in on these. She asked questions that reminded me of F. E. McGahan. Her mind was also a chisel, etching from what I said the most valuable elements and channeling those into the pencil with which she furiously took notes. If I had spent the rest of my life giving lectures to groups that she was in, I would have been happy.

The next time the group brought their children to do activities in the lab, they arrayed themselves at the different stations in the activity room, one parent to a station, with the children moving between the stations, the same as always. Beverley—it turned out her name was Beverley—was positioned at the other end of the room. As always, I started my circuit with the parent closest to me, working with him and his child, slowly working my way from station to station, toward the one where she was positioned. She was as intent in the activity room as she was in the lecture, and she was also incredibly warm, correcting the mistakes the child made and coaxing him to do better work in a gentle, nurturing way. Her seven-year-old daughter was at another station, and I asked her how many children she had. She said nine. I was perplexed, but I didn't pursue it. I did my best to focus on the work we were doing.

The next time she was at the lab, I made my way to where she was working, waited while she finished giving instructions to the child she was working with, and then asked her how she could have nine children when her daughter was only seven. It was a week later; I'd been mulling it over in my mind for a week. She smiled and explained that she took care of six children so their mothers could work. She thought it was better to care for those children and be with her own all the time they were home and out of school. She made a little money that way. When she had spare time, she made a little more editing and polishing poorly written academic papers. But she said she couldn't bring herself to go out and get a professional job when her children were young.

The mystery of the nine children was solved, but then I had something else to think about for the whole weekend. She'd said she polished poorly written academic papers. I wrote poorly written academic papers. I didn't actually admit to myself that I was conspiring to spend more time with her, but it seemed like a match made in heaven. And she did have that beautiful walk...

One day I asked her and her daughter to join me for a cup of coffee. I asked as casually as I could. Then I stood there as casually as I could through a silence that seemed to last forever. Finally, she agreed and, over coffee, her thoughts and insights on my program started to pour out. She told me about the successes her daughter was beginning to have. She told me about working with her nine children at home and the improvements she was seeing there. We talked, and time flew by, and when she left, my mind was buzzing with new ideas.

Beverley was and remains one of those rare creatures who, when she believes in something, latches onto it with her whole being. She has one of the most active minds I've ever encountered, and it is a clear, focused, pragmatic mind. At that time, I was still putting together a puzzle that had a lot of missing pieces at its center. I knew that what I was doing worked. I knew I was accomplishing my most important goal: teaching learning-disabled children how to read. But I didn't know exactly why it worked. Sometimes when I talked, even I didn't understand what I was saying. She had a way of distilling it that made it easier to think about.

For the rest of the time that she and her daughter were in the group, I took advantage of every opportunity for conversation I could get. I asked her questions. Invariably, the answers provoked in my mind more active and exciting thoughts. As the end of the program began to loom, it occurred to me that the next group was going to be very different. Something would be missing. Still telling myself that my motives were purely professional, I asked her to have dinner with me the evening of the last Wednesday lecture. This time, there was no uncomfortable, lingering silence. This time she said yes immediately.

The movies have given us many romantic scenes, some of them vivid and full of feeling, but in my mind they all pale in comparison to the walk Beverley and I took from the College of Optometry to my car that evening. It was professional. It couldn't be anything else. We drove to an inexpensive little restaurant nearby; it was nothing special, typical of the kinds of places that surround university campuses. We had a piece of cheesecake, far too much coffee, and a long conversation about the physical foundations of human intelligence. There were no violins. There were no fireworks. The candles burning on the tables were cheap, and the tablecloths were checkered vinyl, not white linen. But Beverley had a wonderful glow about her; she spoke with enthusiasm; and her presence energized that little restaurant. Every aspect of that evening in that little restaurant is burned into my mind, and the memory has more elegance than any romantic enclave in Paris, Rome, or Barcelona.

And then it was over. We drove back to the university in silence. I walked her from my car to hers. We said a cordial goodnight that we thought was goodbye: it was the end of the program, and there was no reason for her to come back to the university. I shook her hand, and for a moment we lingered, touching just like that. And then she got into her VW bus and drove off into the night.

Some time later, she started taking early childhood education courses at the university, and once again she appeared at the College of Optometry. She was trying to arrange to have her class observe what I was doing with learning-disabled children, and her professor, who was not a fan of my work, wasn't willing to arrange it herself. Beverley was frustrated: the professor had never actually taught; her ideas sounded good academically, but they didn't translate to what the students, most of whom were kindergarten teachers doing recertification courses, knew about living, breathing children. I let her vent. It was a breath of fresh air.

And then she told me that she had been working with children using my program. She wanted to set up a satellite program at the school her daughter attended. She told me about some successes. She told me about her insights. Once again, that razor-sharp mind of hers began cutting away the fat from my thinking. It wasn't a long conversation, but it left me feeling reinvigorated. It must have done something for her as well because she became a regular visitor to the College of Optometry. I went to her daughter's school, and I watched her interacting with, observing, and training children. She was perhaps the best therapist I had ever seen. We became friends. And one day, casually, I mentioned that I could use help with the editing of some poorly written academic papers. There was another silence, and although I didn't know it then, she had cut through the fat in other thoughts of mine as well, and she was considering a question much larger than an editing job. Luckily, once again, she said yes.

What I had in mind was a book that would set down a foundation for performing the activities I had developed. She started out as an editor, but her talents went far beyond that, and when the book was finally done, she was its co-author.

Throughout the evolution of the activities, I had been grappling with two ends of a rope. One was the practical, classroom or therapy room application: activities that could be performed and that would get a result. The other was the theoretical, conceptual end: what it was that was making those activities effective, and that end was still impossible to nail down. This was still the 1960s. Brain mapping hadn't begun yet. The brain was a frontier, like outer space or the inside of an atom. It was constantly offering up new information to science, but it was still mostly a mystery.

Beverley found the theoretical aspect of it fascinating, and she didn't shy away from discussing it. But she really only cared about the practical end. She didn't let the mysteries distract her from the fact that a set of activities had helped her daughter, that they could help other children, and that the better those activities were, the more effectively they would help. Everything I came up with, she improved. When I spent days frustrated by missing puzzle pieces, she brought my mind back to the task at hand: fixing what was wrong with these children. I did my best to remain professional, but every Wednesday morning, when we did a working session before her class, I became more amazed by her brilliance, and every Wednesday after lunch, when she set off across the campus, I was reminded of her walk.

Bringing the Focus Home

The culture of conflict at the College of Optometry was reaching a boiling point. I have a deficit when it comes to accepting that certain kind of criticism that serves only to deflate someone else's ideas, without advancing any theory to replace them. It is a valuable and important part of the academic process; it is part of the system of checks and balances that keeps wild and potentially destructive ideas contained. Even though the rational part of me knows this, that kind of criticism has always seemed to me both cowardly and arrogant, and it has always made me angry.

I was enduring a bout of just that kind of criticism from the leading professor in the College's other theoretical trench. He was determined to undermine my ideas, and it was starting to look like my job was in jeopardy. I was losing sleep. I was questioning myself and my work. And the worst part of it was that, in one way, he was right: I didn't know what was behind it all. I didn't know how the brain worked. I saw that orchestra of forces. I saw how the body responded to them. I knew that the brain responded to them. But I didn't know why. I entered a horrible, dark frame of mind, and I began to wonder whether there was a point in even writing the book at all.

I don't know what I saw, exactly, in Beverley's eyes, but I think it was anger. At that professor. At me for letting him sow the seeds of doubt. At something. Her eyes were bright and passionate. Her body was tense with concentrated energy and emotion. She paused a minute before speaking. Then she let me have it with both barrels.

She had listened to everything I'd said since the first lecture she'd attended. She knew my work as well as I did, probably better. Systematically, she set about unraveling my doubts. She pointed out that what we were dealing with was physics, more than anything. We were dealing with the way the body moves in three-dimensional space. We were dealing with the idea that the foundation of intelligence was rooted in the body's relation to three-dimensional space, time, and energy. She pointed out that among the parents whose children had come through the program were NASA scientists, technological innovators, one theoretical physicist, and many engineers—people who were at the top of their fields in the physical sciences. They hadn't tried to poke holes in what I was saying. They'd understood it because it fit with their understanding and because, regardless of what I said their children were getting better. "That's what it's all about," she said finally. "That those children succeed."

I didn't have any resolve left. I took her in my arms. She resisted a little, but then she bent into my embrace, and we have held each other like that for thirty-five years and counting.

Beverley has played a vital role in discovering the key to the treatment of learning disabilities. First, a man changes when he falls in love. There is a special energy, part showing off and part euphoria, that drives him to run out and slay whatever dragons stand in his way. Beverley and I connected because we shared an interest in treating these children, she because two of her children were learning disabled and me for the host of reasons I have outlined so far. That topic, our work on the book, and our increasing teamwork setting up training programs, solidified our relationship. And so the burst of euphoric energy that comes naturally with falling in love was channeled into this work.

Second, Beverley is smarter than me. My mind tends to grapple with the abstract, to swim in a sea of half-formed concepts, while hers works like a kiln, taking those concepts and firing them into solid, usable shapes. Third, my first impression was correct: she is the best therapist I have ever met. As a result, she always thinks from the standpoint of a therapist. Big ideas and explanations are good to think about and enjoyable to discuss, but it is the experience, the progress, and the success of a child that matters.

In the more than thirty-five years that we have been married, science has redefined the brain. We were developing a robust picture in those classrooms and offices during the 1960s, but we lacked so much knowledge of the physical makeup, processes, and development of the brain that our most maverick ideas were, at best, shots in the dark. It was always frustrating to try to understand and to confront a wall of missing information. My zeal for knowing was stymied again and again, and if it hadn't been for Beverley's strength, passion, courage, and practicality, I can't honestly say that I would have kept going.

Chapter 18:

THE END OF A DREAM

I did keep going. But there was a light turned on in Houston. It burned brightly for a while. And then it went out.

Parents of children with learning disabilities and the teachers and therapists who really want to make a difference in the lives and learning experiences of these children must navigate a confusing labyrinth of conflicting ideas and special interests. Different practitioners give them different answers because the various disciplines try to answer the whole question from just one perspective—their own. Popular buzzwords circulate; some of which seem to mean more than they do. Drugs have been developed, promoted, and prescribed to treat disabilities like Attention Deficit Disorder. With big money behind them, their proliferation has been frightening. Because learning disabilities are complicated, their definitions have changed repeatedly over the years, making solid information harder and harder to find.

To this day, I believe that if the culture created by Dr. Pfeiffer at the College of Optometry had survived, if the nucleus of minds that had evolved in Houston had continued to grow, and if we had continued to take strides forward, including more disciplines in our integrated concept of intelligence, we would have arrived at a comprehensive theory that would have had profound implications. Sadly, it did not.

I am not one to dwell on the negative. Perhaps it didn't happen because it simply was not yet time for it to happen. But there are three episodes, which I believe illustrate how the discoveries made by a diligent and maverick group, discoveries that changed the lives of thousands of children, did not become common knowledge.

It Takes More Than Money

The first real blow to the work we were doing should have been the boon we needed to advance at an even more rapid rate. We got funding.

The Perceptual Motor and Visual Perception Lab at the university was getting real results. Satellite programs around the city were changing children's lives. Our thinking was expanding; the activities we had developed were getting more acute; and our ideas were gaining traction. In only a few short years, I went from watching Edward make his noble walk to the front of the assembly to speaking in front of standing-room-only audiences of hundreds of interested people. One day when I was at home, Dr. Pfeiffer called me excitedly and told me to turn on the television. I did, and there we were. The local station was airing a one-hour show featuring a program we had set up in a school in Spring Branch, a suburb of Houston. This was back in the days when there were only a few channels, so being featured on TV was a big deal. We were definitely getting somewhere.

Then word came that the Texas State Legislature was planning to invest millions of dollars to conduct research and to establish programs for learning-disabled children. Our first reaction was euphoric. We were going to get the resources we needed to make things happen. We were going to be able to bring all the disciplines together. We were going to be able to work on a grand scale. We imagined how many children we would help. The opportunity was staggering.

At that time, I lived in LaPorte, just two blocks away from the water. When I had something to think about, I'd take a walk from my house down to the ship channel to watch the yachts and the freighters floating past, to watch the sunlight flicker on the water, to look up into the stars that our space rockets were trying to reach, and to allow what was spinning in my mind to spread out into all that wide open space. The day I heard about what the Legislature was planning, I was so happy I couldn't sit still. That evening, I walked down to the water to think about all the marvelous things those resources could make possible.

I was so very, very naïve. I was aware of politics, but I certainly wasn't savvy. I knew there were battles surrounding the work we were doing, and I definitely knew that the clash of ideas at the College of Optometry sometimes heated up to a boil but, for the most part, I hadn't been the one on the front lines of those battles. Jack Harris, Chester Pfeiffer, and many others had fought them for me. While I understood that what we were doing was outside of the establishment and that the establishment resisted it, it was unfathomable to me that, now that the Legislature was planning to support our work, we would still have to fight. In my mind, the government's support would validate what we were doing, would help us to evolve, and would give our efforts the vote of confidence they needed to gain broad acceptance.

That evening I didn't brace myself for a struggle. I thought up research projects to do. I didn't ready myself to bicker and fight over every dollar. I imagined the children we would help. I didn't think strategically. I thought idealistically.

Then an important politician flew in from Austin to discuss plans for using these newly allocated resources. I went to meet with him as a kind of representative of the group I was working with. Other influential people were present, including well-respected leaders in education and academics. It started out positive, exciting, and as idealistic as my dreams, but I will never forget the sinking feeling that grew in my stomach as the meeting progressed. Suddenly, there was a stack of money on the table, and everything changed. We talked about children with learning disabilities, but we weren't talking about children, and we weren't talking about learning disabilities: we were talking about that stack of money. We were talking about funding departments, about expanding programs, about the *administration* of education, about the *theory* of education, but, ultimately, not at all about the basic operating principle of education: that children are supposed to learn.

The kids who needed help got lost in the fray. The funding was absorbed.

Politics in Academia

Some time later, Dr. Pfeiffer's health began to deteriorate, and the culture of conflict he had created and fostered at the College of Optometry began to spin out of control.

Today, Vision Development is a well established sub-profession within optometry, and it is generally agreed that visual exercises can have a dramatic impact on a wide variety of visual impairments. Back then, however, there was great resistance to that idea. Optometry was a specific discipline focused on the diagnosis of visual problems and the prescription of corrective mechanisms, most often lenses. The vanguard in optometry wanted to keep it that way. It was an uphill battle even for Dr. Pfeiffer, with his impeccable credentials and a lifetime of accomplishment, to shelter our fledgling ideas. During one of his recuperations from illness, the dam broke.

I am the first to admit that my understanding of the theory behind my approach is a work in progress. The practical application, however, is fundamentally effective. Using the program I had developed at that time, I could take almost any individual, test his vision, give him activities to do for fifteen minutes, and show, upon retesting, a pronounced improvement in his vision. Even most people who disagreed wholeheartedly with my explanations were at least intrigued by that. It was, after all, a measurable, observable fact.

But the man who was named Interim Dean when Dr. Pfeiffer left to recuperate was one of the staunchest critics of the work we were doing on the developmental side of the culture of conflict. His resistance was so firm, in fact, that he refused even to look at the program. He refused to read the papers we wrote. He refused to give us and our work the time of day.

On the day he was named Interim Dean, he made his first ever visit to my lab. I was working with a child, who was lying down on the floor tracking a noise-emitting pendulum ball swinging from the ceiling above him. The new Interim Dean walked over to us, and as I turned to greet him and to try my best to offer my congratulations for his promotion, he grabbed the pendulum ball by the string, yanked it out of the ceiling, and announced that what we were doing was beneath the profession of optometry. That was that.

What had, for years, been a tolerable level of conflict between professionals escalated into war. It's one thing to ignore people who are passionate about what they're doing; it's quite another to attack them. Ignoring them builds tension and mutual resentment. It creates a powder keg. The attack sets that powder keg off, and all hell breaks loose. That is what happened while Dr. Pfeiffer recuperated.

The Interim Dean and his backers were among the elite of the optometric community. They had their own credentials, and now they had the added clout of the dean's office. We had our faith, our increasing list of results, and the parents whose children we had helped. It wasn't a fair fight.

But word spread and, for a brief period, the administration was inundated with a show of support for our work. Dr. Pfeiffer made angry phone calls from his sickbed. Teachers from schools all around Houston, who had seen students in their classes improve after taking part in our programs, sent letters. Therapists, who had incorporated some of what we were doing into their own practices, spoke up. Most of the support, though, came from the parents whose flesh and blood had been helped by what we were doing. Luckily, some of them had some real influence. Some were NASA scientists. Some were well-regarded doctors. Some were businessmen in the community; some of them were also university donors, which really mattered to the administration. All these people raised a ruckus, and that ruckus was the only thing that kept our Lab alive.

The Lab survived Dr. Pfeiffer's absence from the university, but something in the air had changed. In those months, the vitality in the conflict that Dr. Pfeiffer had worked so hard to create, develop, and maintain had evaporated. Resentment took its place. On both sides of the conflict, the hard fight had hardened us into our trenches, and one by one, those of us on the developmental side of the battle started looking elsewhere to pursue our work. Dr. Pfeiffer went on to become Dean of the newly founded Oklahoma College of Optometry in Tahlequah. Some of the faculty moved with him. Some went elsewhere.

It was hard for me to leave. By then, I had tenure, so at least my job wasn't on the line. I also had a two-year waiting list for the Perceptual Motor and Visual Perception Lab, and I knew that if I left it would eventually disappear. Still, working life in the College of Optometry grew increasingly untenable. The conflict was no longer productive for any of us on either side of the old battle. Before too long, the nucleus of great minds that had come together to solve the problems of the learning disabled began to drift apart.

Political Money Troubles

At one point, it seemed as though another nucleus was forming, and it seemed as though we might be able to pick up where we left off. The gravitational center of this second nucleus was a place called Pacific States University in Southern California.

Pacific States didn't have an accredited doctoral program in education but, as the administration worked to create one, it sponsored a network of some of the most dynamic and committed minds in the field. Ralph

Schrock, Lou Ellen Tomlinson, and Mary Meeker: these were pioneers in their fields. They were well respected. They were highly accomplished. They created another fascinating clique of creativity and insight, and once again I found myself in a blossoming garden of ideas.

I've talked to other people about their doctoral work, and I can't imagine any program as challenging or as engaging as the one offered by Pacific States. It was a small program, and I developed meaningful relationships with all the program advisors, many of which matured into lifelong friendships. My work with the integration of physical dynamics and intellectual ability was the core of my thesis, and my advisors challenged me at every step, forcing me to think further, cutting away my bad ideas, and most importantly allowing themselves to become intimately and emotionally involved in the work.

The program lasted for three vibrant, energetic years. My relationships with my advisors, the reams of new information I poured into my mind, and my continued successes working with learning-disabled children fueled a burst of progress similar to my early days in Houston. During this period, I refined the activities I had developed; they became part of a larger framework called "intelligence development" or "intelligence education." I still didn't know exactly what was at the core of it all, but the practical application continued to evolve.

The program's accreditation was slow in coming, but none of us were worried about that. The university's administration was committed to providing a good education and we knew from the outset that the accreditation process would probably take nearly as long as the program itself. During those three years, it didn't occur to any of us that there would be any problem.

Then, just before graduation, the President of the University, on what must have been one of the most painful days of his career, told us that we each needed to "donate" $10,000 to a certain high-ranking California lawmaker to "grease the gears" of accreditation. That lawmaker knew the time, energy, and money that we had invested. He knew the value of the degree we had pursued. He stood in the way because he thought we would find a way to come up with the money.

But it was a lot of money, and we couldn't do it. Had it survived, the Pacific States doctoral program in education would probably have contributed greatly to the quality of education that American students receive. It was stopped, however, with tragic finality, by a powerful politician with sticky fingers.

Closing the Doors on Academia

For me, the Pacific States experience was the final straw. I left academia. I knew that if I could get people together in a group, if I could demonstrate to them that their reading, vision, and physical organization would improve after fifteen minutes of activity, I would still be able to help children. I also knew that my way of thinking and my idealism were incompatible with the traditional academic environment. I went on the lecture circuit, and I left the university campuses behind.

Together, these episodes also illustrate why it is so difficult for parents, teachers, and therapists to get a clear picture of how to help a learning-disabled child. Amid the great ideas and the great passion of those people, there exist chasms defined more by politics than by purpose, more by special interest than by specific need, and more by what looks good than by what is good.

That doesn't mean the solutions aren't out there—they are—and with commitment, discretion, and common sense, they can be found.

Chapter 19:

THE PACIFIC NORTHWEST

In 1975, Beverley and I moved to Port Angeles, Washington, a small seaside town on the Olympic Peninsula just west of Seattle. It is a quiet town in one of the most picturesque parts of the world, nestled between the rugged peaks of the Olympic Mountains and the placid waters of the Strait of Juan de Fuca, and in the 1970s, it was a destination for artists, thinkers, and escapists of all kinds, many of whom had cast their gaze away from the big cities in the hopes of finding something they had known in the sixties and lost.

I was forty-four and Beverley was thirty-four when we decided to have children together. We each had three children from our previous marriages, and the three we had together created a real-life version of *The Brady Bunch*. Only the Belgau Bunch was slightly different: from the very beginning, our combined household was full of highly intelligent, passionate people committed to pushing the envelope—usually in three to five different directions at once.

It was a uniquely stimulating environment—for me, maybe, more than for anyone else in the house. When I had begun to study learning disabilities, my older children were already past their early childhood. Through my professional career, I had worked mainly with elementary- and middle school-aged children, and I had not had the opportunity to observe firsthand, from the standpoint of a body of knowledge, the rapid, surprising development of very young children. Seeing them acquire basic physical capabilities, seeing them learn and grow, gave me a whole new insight into the basic operating principles of early development.

Also, the three children Beverley and I had together did not have learning disabilities. They were all prodigious in academic work, even from an early age, and yet they still improved incrementally as they used the Learning Breakthrough Program. I began to see that the same activities that were effective for learning-disabled children were also effective for very bright, successful children. The scope of what I was trying to grasp began to expand.

I maintained close friendships with most of my advisors from Pacific States. It wasn't their fault that the political system was corrupt; they were as upset by what had happened as I was; and their commitment to working with and helping children was both inspiring and instructive. Two of them, especially, became pillars in the next phase of my life.

Dr. Ralph Schrock was one of the pioneers in the field of Vision Development. Members of the optometric profession recognized him as the authority on the processes of developing binocular visual skills, eliminating amblyopia (lazy eye), and correcting strabismus (crossed eyes) with training rather than surgery. He had his optometry practice in La Jolla, next to the main campus of the University of California, San Diego, and there he experimented with a whole range of exercises to improve vision. Like Dr. Koetting, Dr. Schrock was a dreamer, and his dream was to develop a therapeutic program that would all but replace eyeglasses. It was a dream he chased with vigor and thoughtfulness, and he could always be counted on for a late-night phone conversation or a piece of inspiration when I needed it.

Another was Dr. Mary Meeker. She was an energetic, magnetic woman, full of energy, who had studied the groundbreaking research completed by Dr. J. P. Guilford during World War II, which had defined intelligence far more broadly and completely than any other program had done before it. Dr. Guilford's work postulated 120 factors of human intelligence, of which twenty-six related to academic success. From his closer look at intelligence, he had determined that each of those factors could be learned, creating a school of thought called "Intelligence Education" that survives even today. He had said "Intelligence education is intelligent education," a catch-phrase that became a sort of motto for us in our work.

Because each of the factors could be learned, Dr. Meeker saw an opportunity to create a comprehensive testing and training system. She focused on the twenty-six factors related to academic success, and she developed a model of academic intelligence known as the Structure of Intellect (SOI).

SOI evolved to become an extremely powerful tool on two counts. First, it produced a testing regimen that didn't reduce IQ to a simple number, but which defined intelligence in terms of relative ability over a broad spectrum of attributes. A standard IQ test provides some insight and can be, to an extent, a predictor of success in school and work, but with SOI testing, Dr. Meeker could see into the mechanics of the mind. An individual might be very poor at remembering numbers, for example, but might be extremely good at spatial sequencing. An individual terrible at mastering comparative puzzles might prove to be highly creative. This enabled the second benefit: using this high resolution picture of the individuals' strengths and weaknesses, Dr. Meeker designed programs for improving ability across the whole structure. By using the stronger areas to reinforce and develop the weaker ones, the SOI training programs could enable the individual to make the most of all of his skills.

Dr. Meeker and Dr. Schrock were both early believers in what I was doing, and while I was still their student, they both incorporated my balance and spatial training tools into their training programs. Dr. Meeker found that, when she used my program in conjunction with her own training modules, her patients improved at a dramatically faster rate. For Dr. Schrock, my work became a central part of his Vision Development regimen. He was a meticulous observer, and he found that of all the activities he was doing, my tools produced the fastest and most lasting improvements.

Shortly after we moved to the Northwest, I also met Dr. Jerry Winger, a devotee of Dr. Meeker who was then running the learning disabilities program for the Seattle public schools. That relationship launched another training program at University Heights elementary, near the University of Washington, and it also introduced me to yet another creative, compassionate human being. One of the first things I noticed about Dr. Winger was that his emotions ran close to the surface. Good music and a child's success always brought tears to his eyes, and although his hands were, in many ways, tied by politics in many ways during his time at the school district, he remained an advocate for children throughout his life.

I also became close friends with another escapee from the big cities, a marine biologist and environmental scientist named Walt Pearson.

Walt is a scientist's scientist, from his slow, careful style of speech to his neatly trimmed beard to his safari hats to the meticulous way that his mind works. Marine biology is, necessarily, an extremely meticulous discipline; it requires the careful accumulation of vast quantities of data which have to be correct if any reasonable conclusions are to be drawn from them. And Walt is a genuine truth-seeker; he is passionately determined to see what is there, a focus that has sometimes, since marine biology touches on highly sensitive environmental issues, made him unpopular with those who want the workings of the world to support their politics.

As our friendship grew, it became evident that Walt and I are very different sorts of people. For me, in understanding there is always the energy of invention; seeing a problem is a catalyst for solving it, and that energy takes over as soon as the problem becomes evident. For Walt, the joy is in discovering what is there. Soon after we met, we began spending a great number of evenings sitting, talking, sharing notes on our projects, and thinking together, from our two different points of view, on a whole range of subjects.

These four unique individuals, along with Beverley, formed the gridiron of the next phase of my life.

New Steps in Another Direction

My project was this. I had been working with children, experimenting, improving my programs on the fly, inventing new tools, discarding the ones that didn't work, keeping the ones that did, and learning at a rapid rate. I had been driven by excitement, by necessity, and by the progressive advancement of the groups in Houston and Southern California. I had also been driven by my own lack of knowledge. When Lois had first brought her students into my arts and crafts class, I hadn't known a single thing about the mechanics of the brain, about learning disabilities, or about the systems of perceptual-motor functioning. I'd been an aircraft mechanic hastily prepared for the classroom, and because my work with learning-disabled children had progressed so rapidly, I had spent most of my time trying to catch up.

By 1975, I was no longer trying to fill in the gaps in my knowledge. I was pushing against the edge of what science knew about the human brain. I didn't have the same pressures that I'd had at the university. Rather than working at a frenzied pace in the training environments, I could work more slowly, think more methodically, and develop a structure for everything I had been doing.

The first part of that structure was brought into focus by Dr. Schrock.

He had seen that while students demonstrated an immediate, observable improvement after using my training program, that improvement only became permanent from repeated work. Because of my background, I'd designed my program of activities for classroom and therapy room environments, which meant a great variety of exercises requiring a lot of apparatus. Dr. Schrock challenged me to create a program that would deliver the best of what I had learned and developed, but that could be used at home, and that could be sold for a price that wouldn't break the bank.

The second part of the structure was the theoretical explanation. Somehow, I had to put together all the phenomena I had observed, all the improvements I had seen, all the data I had gathered from books and lectures and conversations, and wrap that up into a cohesive picture that would explain why human balance plays such a dynamic role in intelligence, learning, and the quality of our lives.

I started with the program of activities, which Dr. Schrock, Beverley, and I named the Learning Breakthrough Program.

Chapter 20:

THE VARIABLE DIFFICULTY BALANCE PLATFORM

The Variable Difficulty Balance Platform, or Balance Board, was the first piece of equipment that went into the Learning Breakthrough Program, and for good reason. Simple as it is, the Balance Board is perhaps the most profound tool for refining the fundamental processes that provide either a foundation for intellection achievement or an impediment.

The Balance Board evolved dramatically through the years, from a piece of wood balanced on its center point to a much more sophisticated device. That evolution occurred along the same lines as all the rest of my research: I would think of hundreds of possibilities, I would try any that seemed reasonable, and I would keep only those that produced an immediate, observable improvement. That process took something that had colloquial support in the early 1960s and turned it into a powerful tool for learning enhancement.

When I first started to work with the physical component of balance, before I joined the University of Houston in their College of Optometry and before I had any idea what I was doing, balance stimulation systems in general—and balance boards in particular—were already being used with some success. Although balance stimulation therapies had not gained any sort of universal approval or acceptance as a remedy for learning disabilities, they were used to enhance balance in young children, and they were used relatively widely in physical rehabilitation. When I came across the idea, it looked good enough to try in my own laboratory. The day I tried it was one of the most important turning pointsof my professional life.

At that point, the children in my classroom were already working with pendulum balls, as we had found them to have a positive impact on oral reading skills. The students were instructed to stand in a certain place and direct the motion of the pendulum ball through space, sometimes over a target and sometimes in various directions, as directed by a spotter. They would hit the ball with their hands, or they would use the Visual Motor Control Stick to direct the trajectory of the ball. I made some balance boards, and I had the children stand on them while performing this activity. The results were profound. In many of the children, the addition of the balance board made such a significant and obvious difference that I felt as though lightning had struck. It immediately became a central feature of the training in that classroom, and my success with it was a large part of the reason that I was hired to run the lab at the university, and allowed to run my various training programs outside the university as well.

It was because of those training programs that I made one of the most significant refinements to the Balance Board. I got along well with the children under my care, but part of the deficiency imposed by most learning disabilities is a difficulty in following directions, and the children in my classrooms were no exception. For the most part, they did what I told them, but they did not always do it *how* I told them to do it. There was, without a doubt, considerable variance in the attention given to the activities among the students. There was also considerable variance in the results that they achieved. I assumed there was a correlation: that the children who did the activities correctly got the most out of them, and the children who did them incorrectly got the least out of them.

Consequently, when I started at the university and launched my training program, I was most adamant that the activities be done by the book. In that regard, I had considerably more success in this environment. The participants were there because they *wanted* to be there. The parents came with their children and were present to see how things should be done. And the program was operated under the auspices of a highly respected university; that endorsement alone gave my instructions more weight. Also, a number of influential scientists, including one of the astronauts' doctors, brought their children through the program. This, of course, was when America was looking at the stars and NASA was the Camelot of scientific genius, part of the folklore of the nation. The people who were putting a man on the moon were highly regarded and highly respected, and when one of them had a child in the program and was intent on following my instructions, you can bet all the other parents followed suit. That was wonderful. I finally had what I wanted: everybody performing the activities I had designed exactly as I had designed them and exactly as I instructed.

A Balancing Act Perfected

Still, there was one small problem. The activities were not as effective as I thought they would be. The results were profound for some children. They were marginal for others. I realized, painfully, that it was not just that the more attentive children achieved a greater benefit. There was something wrong with the structure of the activities themselves.

Finally, after a period of worry and frustration, I made an interesting observation. While some of the children naturally stood on the Balance Board with their bodies centered and with their feet straight and evenly spaced on either side of the center line, most of them stood askew. Their bodies favored one side or the other. One foot turned out. Their posture on the Balance Board reflected their normal posture, which for many learning-disabled children was part of the problem. Most importantly, I noticed that *the effectiveness of the program seemed to mirror the level to which the child was centered on the Balance Board.*

To solve this problem, I placed a grid on the top of the board, and from then on, the primary instruction in every training sequence was, "Stand on the Balance Platform with your feet equal distance from the center line and your toes lined up." In other words, stand square on the board. In retrospect, it seems intuitively obvious that unless an individual is centered, the balance board actually becomes an *un*balance board: instead of correcting the inefficiencies that contribute to postural problems and learning deficiencies, the board actually reinforces those inefficiencies.

Once I put the grid on the board and made sure that everybody using it lined themselves up according to that grid, its effectiveness skyrocketed. No longer was improvement limited to those who lined themselves up naturally. Now everybody, from the learning-disabled children to their acclaimed scientist parents, would see a marked improvement in key areas of information processing after performing a sequence of activities on the Balance Board.

It is a maxim of therapy that improvement occurs at the breaking point. Therefore, as an individual's ability to perform an activity improves, it is necessary to increase the difficulty of the activity. Knowing this, I spent a lot of time and energy working on ways to increase the difficulty of balancing on the Balance Board. This gave rise to the second important innovation, the variable-difficulty rockers.

Initially, I made a set of rockers for each balance board that consisted of various pairs of rockers with different radii. This made it possible to increase the difficulty level of the Balance Board, but it was also laborious: you had to unscrew one set of rockers and screw on another set in order to change the difficulty level, and most people would rather just leave the balance level the same rather than going to all that trouble. I puzzled over this dilemma. I wanted the Balance Board to be as effective as possible, and to address as wide a variety of needs as possible, but it also had to be easy to use or people just wouldn't use it. Finally, I had another eureka moment.

It happened while I was on a long, hard seminar tour. I had been driving for ten hours through dense fog, which required me to concentrate on the road at all times, and when I lay down to sleep I could still see the road's center lines flashing like strobe lights through my vision. I had also been thinking, while I was driving, about how to change the balance level of the balance board without having so many rockers, and the two visual images crossed and blended together in my exhausted mind.

I visualized the image of a silhouette. It had a big, two-dimensional circle slowly rotating on its north/south axis. As the circle rotated, it took on an oval, elliptical shape. The radius north/south axis remained constant while the east/west axis decreased until it became a single line, running along the flashing image of the highway's median. That flashing center line finally put me to sleep, and when I awoke the next morning, I had my answer.

I could make rockers that rotated on a fixed center. The rockers would rotate exactly on the north/south axis, and the length of that axis would remain constant because the center of the rocker would be fixed. However, as they rotated, they would change the effective radius of the rocker. The effective curve, which defined the difficulty level of the balance board, would sharpen with the rotation of the rockers in exactly the same way that the curve of the ellipse sharpened as the circle rotated in my mind.

Kent Brauninger, a mathematician living in Port Angeles, provided a formula to use to determine the effective radius of the rocker at each angle of rotation, and I began to print a grid onto the bottoms of the boards as well as on the tops. While the top grid helped the user align his feet and toes, the bottom grid allowed the user to ensure the rockers remained parallel; ; if the rockers were not parallel, the effective radius of the rockers wouldn't match, and it would no longer be a balance board.

The new balance board, with the grid on the top to keep the user in balance and the variable difficulty rockers, became an extremely effective part of my program.

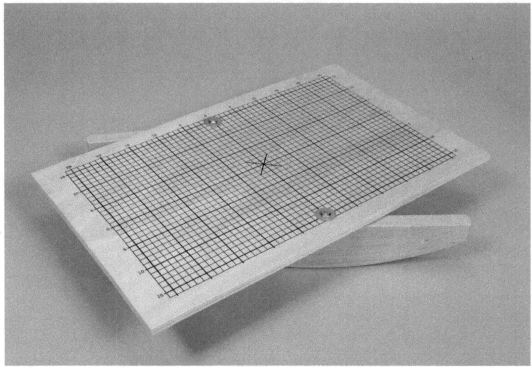

Variable Difficulty Belgau Balance Board ™

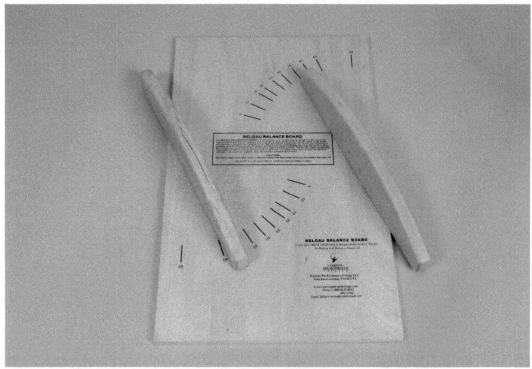

Variable Difficulty Belgau Balance Board ™

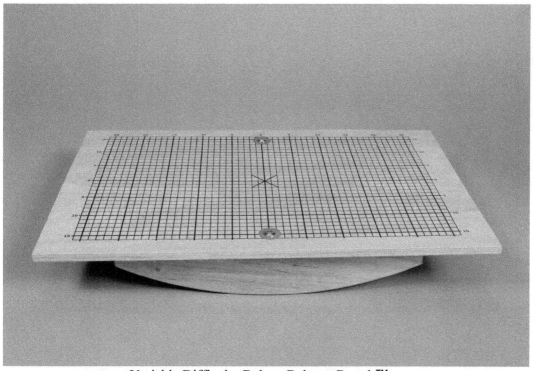

Variable Difficulty Belgau Balance Board ™

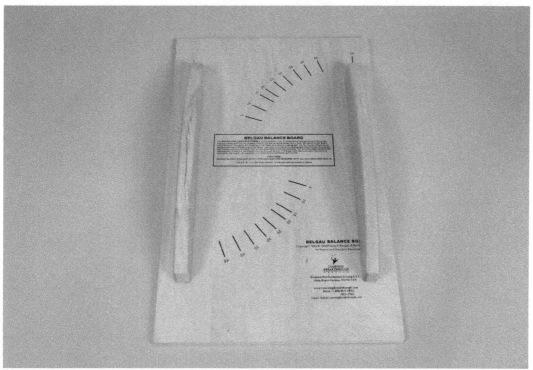

Variable Difficulty Belgau Balance Board ™

Chapter 21:

TOOLS OF THE TRADE

The Balance Board would be the foundation of the Learning Breakthrough Program. The other equipment that I added to it would enable children to perform various activities. The goal of all of these activities was to exercise the body's multisensory interaction with three-dimensional space and with gravity, and so I gave considerable thought to the dynamics of the three-dimensional world. Which pieces of equipment would I include in the kit in order to ensure that the greatest possible number of the basic processes for orientation and operation in three-dimensional physical space would be exercised?

Once again, I went back to the lessons I learned in Mr. Royer's classroom, to the challenge he had given us to determine what calibrated the swinging of a pendulum. Since then, I had had my first real success when my students had used a pendulum ball hung from the ceiling in the classroom, directing its motion with a striped bat in order to get it to swing over a target. As I was putting the kit together, I gave further thought to the physical processes that were at work in this exercise.

The pendulum expresses some of the most basic principles of the physical universe. It is calibrated to the acceleration of gravity; it always responds according to the force that is exerted on it; and an individual's ability to control its motion precisely is both a gauge and an exercise of his relationship to three-dimensional space. As a result, what seems like a remarkably simple task—tracking the ball through space, determining when to intercept it, how much force to exert upon it to put it on a new path, and

123

how to create the new path to get it to go over a target—actually requires high-level calculus, vector analysis, and an application of all the physical laws of motion.

I had always been fascinated by the "finesse component" when I had watched the children I worked with playing with a pendulum ball. At first, in almost all cases (including children who were athletically gifted), it was as if the computations were not being performed quickly enough. The children would either hesitate while the ball was swinging back to them, then respond abruptly and with too much force, or they would be over-eager, beginning the process of hitting the ball too early and being off-balance by the time the ball actually got back to them. Over time, however, as they improved the organization of their brains, their movements, their reactions, and their calculations would all take on a certain finesse. It got to the point where I could almost predict how well-organized a child's brain was by how smoothly he could "dance" with a pendulum ball.

The other advantage of a pendulum ball is that the pendulum's period is constant, regardless of the length of its swing. If you hit the pendulum ball hard, it will go farther in its arc, but it will still return to the starting point in the same period of time that it would have taken if you hit it softly. This means that the pendulum ball enforces a set rhythm on the activities. That rhythm helps to structure the process of neurological organization.

Vestibular Motor Control Stick

The means used to direct the pendulum ball through space are also important. The pendulum ball can be controlled with open palms, fists, elbows, the forehead, with any kind of stick or bat, and so on. Different activities exercise the vestibular-motor relationship with space in different ways, but one of the key dynamics of that relationship that I have always focused on is the integration of the two sides of the body. I designed the "Vestibular Motor Control Stick" with this integration, as well as the need to increase the difficulty of an activity as the child's skill increased, in mind.

The control stick has wide colored bands, separated by narrow black bands, and when using it the child holds the bat with both hands, positioned an equal distance from the center. The first level of the activity is simply to control the motion of the ball through space, without regard to the bands on the stick. Once the child is able to control the ball's motion smoothly, without jerky movements and without hitting the ball too hard, the next level of difficulty is to hit the ball with specific colored bands. After the child masters that, the hitting the ball with the black bands, since they are narrower, increases the difficulty level again. This activity forces the two sides of the body to work together, thus developing integration between the two sides of the body and, as a result, between the two sides of the brain. It also becomes increasingly precise as the child graduates to higher levels of difficulty, honing both bi-lateral integration and interaction with three-dimensional space.

Target Stand and Pins

Using targets adds yet another dimension to the activity. Placed on a flat, elevated stand some distance in front of the child, each target is identified with a different shape—circle, cross, square, triangle, and diamond. The child is instructed to hit the ball so that it swings out and over the top of one of the targets.

This activity serves to bring into focus the child's relationship with three-dimensional space, as the child now contends with the multisensory activity of hitting the ball with the bat, the high-level mathematical calculations required to change and direct the trajectory of the ball, the bi-lateral integration required to precisely maneuver the bat to the appropriate angle with the right amount of force to make the ball go where it is supposed to, and the three-dimensional spatial awareness required to identify a target in space. It seems like an extremely simple activity: a child stands on a balance board and hits a ball over targets with a bat. But in reality, the activity exercises many of the most fundamental processes required for orientation and operation within three-dimensional space, and for higher brain functions such as reading and mathematics.

Chapter 22:

BEAN BAGS

The appropriate bean bag exercises can have a profoundly positive effect, and from the very early days of my research they have been an indispensable part of every training program. Correctly performed, bean bag exercises can promote the integration of the two sides of the body, assist with vision training, and exercise some of our most basic physical processes. I decided to put three bean bags, each a different color and a different weight, in the Learning Breakthrough Program.

The most basic bean bag exercise is to throw the bean bag up in the air with both hands, tracking it with the eyes as it moves through space, and then to catch it with both hands when it comes back down. This activity promotes the integration of the two sides of the body. as the two hands have to work together, with equal force, to throw and catch the bean bag. It promotes the muscular structures responsible for tracking, which can improve vision. It can be further enhanced as a visual exercise: by holding the head straight and tracking the bean bag with the peripheral vision, that visual element is developed. If the child points his or her nose at the bean bag and moves his whole head, keeping his eyes still, it helps to refine the head and neck movements that we use when looking beyond the range of motion of our eyes in their sockets.

The next activity is to throw and catch the bean bag with one hand, track it through space with the eyes, and then catch it with the same hand when it comes back down. This moves the exercise to one side of the body, which in many cases is extremely beneficial. One of my earliest observations was that the learning disabled children with whom I was working would suppress one side of their body. If one side of the body is disorganized, the whole neurological system suffers. Thus, focusing exercise on that side of the body makes intuitive sense.

Once a child is comfortable throwing and catching one bean bag with both hands, and with either hand by itself, the next challenge is to cross the midline by throwing the bean bag from one hand to the other and back again. This means that the "right hand has to know what the left hand is doing," that when the left hand throws the right hand has to be ready to catch. Again, it seems like a simple action, but to perform it smoothly requires the integration of sensory information from both sides of the body, as well as from the visual system. Any activity that crosses the midline of the body also crosses the midline of the brain, increasing the neurological activity required to perform it effectively.

After these three basic activities have been mastered, other activities can be invented. Throwing and catching two, or even three, bean bags increases the difficulty level and the neurological component. Throwing and catching bean bags with a partner adds another dimension to the training. And because the goal of all these activities is to create a high-resolution multisensory operating space, throwing and catching bean bags with the eyes closed dramatically increases the difficulty of the task and makes it a visualization exercise.

Including bean bags in the Learning Breakthrough Program was also a way to add another dimension of exercise to the Program as a whole. The pendulum ball, because it is attached to the ceiling and because its movements are defined by the string, is inherently controlled in a way that bean bag activities are not. The bean bags move freely, so the individual working with them must remain constantly aware in order to continually react appropriately to the imperfections of his own actions.

When a child begins a regimen of activity with bean bags, as with the pendulum ball, his or her movements are typically uncontrolled; as the child progresses with the activity, and as the various systems being exercised come into better harmony, the child's actions become increasingly controlled, allowing the level of difficulty associated with the activity to be increased, thereby providing greater challenge and, as a result, even greater improvement. Generally, people learn and improve best when there are clear-cut rewards for success and clear-cut consequences for failure, and bean bag activities have this reward-and-consequence system built in. The ability to perform an activity well is its own reward; performing it poorly means dropping the bean bag—and nobody wants to drop the bean bag. There is, therefore, a psychological motivation to perform well, which drives the individual to do exactly what will make the activity most effective.

Chapter 23:

THE SUPER BALL TOSS BACK

Throwing and catching an object was a central feature of many of the activities I had developed, whether that object was a bean bag or the pendulum ball. In trying to maximize the diversity of throwing and catching exercises, I began to visualize various types of apparatus to add diversity to the process of controlling the motion of an object through space.

The Toss Back, which consists of an angled platform placed on the ground, with the angle facing toward the child doing activity, "tosses back" the ball thrown against it. In combination with the balance board, this activity complements the pendulum ball and bean bag exercises by providing essentially another dimension of the same general form of activity.

Initially, I debated whether to include the Toss Back in the Learning Breakthrough Program. Some teachers and therapists incorporated it into their training regimens and they reported that it was as effective as the other tools, but it was also another apparatus to manufacture. It was another piece to put in the box. It would take a little longer to manufacture the Learning Breakthrough, and it would have to cost a little more.

But one of the great advantages of the Super Ball Toss Back, which, in my focus on therapeutic effectiveness I hadn't thought enough about, was that it was *fun*. When I used the Toss Back when working with children, it was usually their favorite part of the training. They got to throw a bouncy ball against a board that bounced it back to them. Sometimes they got to throw two balls. Sometimes the balls went all over the place. It was *fun!*

Back in the early days in Houston, we had discovered that one of the keys for good therapeutic programs was to harness the natural energy of the children we were trying to help and to channel that enjoyment into productive activities. The more fun the training could be (as long as the right controls were in place to keep it effective), the better would be our results. If it was fun, the children would buy into the program. If it was effective, the parents would buy in, too. When parents and children agreed on its value, both for purpose and for play, the program was at its most successful.

The Super Ball Toss Back was the final addition to the Learning Breakthrough Program, and when I had all the pieces in place, creating a set of equipment that I knew would create both immediate and lasting improvement, I could hardly wait to show it to Dr. Schrock. It was like that morning in junior high school when I had finally figured out what calibrated the motion of a pendulum and raced to school to tell my answer to Mr. Royer. I knew I had something that could change a person's life. I knew I'd designed it to be cost effective for almost everyone. I was so pleased with the overall program that I scheduled a trip to La Jolla to visit with Dr. Schrock and show him the contents of my box.

Dr. Schrock inspected everything I'd put in the kit. He listened to me explain why each one had been included, and he listened as I explained why other equipment had been left out. He looked through the book of tests I had compiled. He looked through the book of activities. He thought carefully about my rationale. And at the end of it, he looked at me and said, "Well, Frank, I think you've got it."

Chapter 24:

CHANGING LIVES

In the years after I had compiled the Learning Breakthrough Program, a number of events occurred that shaped the way I thought about what I was doing.

First, throughout almost my entire experience with teaching, I had worked with learning-disabled children, and I had been focused on helping them to overcome their disabilities. My own children were not disabled. They were highly gifted, but I still insisted that they use the program, and I noticed improvements. In San Diego, Dr. Schrock incorporated the Learning Breakthrough Program into vision training he was doing with high-level Navy pilots, and he called it the most effective tool in his office. Other developmental optometrists who were using the program in their therapy rooms found that it was effective for patients of all types. And the parents of children who worked with the program, who often did the training with their kids, reported improvements in their professional performance as well as in the academic performance of their children. Because those parents came from diverse backgrounds, their professions covered a broad spectrum of work. The Learning Breakthrough Program seemed to have broader and broader applications.

But my focus, almost to the exclusion of everything else, remained facing the challenges of children who were poor readers, who had difficulty in mathematics, and who struggled in the classroom. I was focused—too focused, perhaps—on their disabilities.

In 1988, Dr. Jim Gage and Dr. Susan Workman, two independent researchers, put together a pilot program in Alpine, TX, to study the effects of the Learning Breakthrough Program's activities on the elderly. They were both highly inquisitive, energetic people, and although they went into the study without any preconceptions, before they started they went out of their way to visit Port Angeles, to sit and talk, and to understand the kind of therapeutic environment they should establish for the study. Although we had known each other before, setting up and executing the study brought us closer, and during that time I invested myself in much more research than I had ever done before regarding the processes of degeneration that accompany increasing age.

Perhaps I was particularly intrigued by this study because I turned 58 that year, and after you turn 50, the approach of each new decade looks a little like a gun barrel. With 60 on the horizon, I was beginning to wonder what was going to happen to *me* on the slippery slope down the other side of "the hill."

The study Jim and Susan conducted was small and simple. They solicited volunteers from the retired community in Alpine, and they filled an experimental group of twelve individuals and a control group of eleven individuals. In both groups, the volunteers were at least 55 years old and in generally good health. The age range of the experimental group was 55 to 89 years old, and the age range of the control group was 56 to 85 years old. Both groups were similar in terms of education and income.

At the beginning of their study, Jim and Susan conducted an extensive battery of tests focusing on visual acuity and functional visual skills. A licensed developmental optometrist conducted exams on all the participants, who were also given tests of visual memory, auditory memory, and visual and auditory processing.

Over the next twelve weeks, each member of the experimental group received two thirty-minute training sessions per week. These sessions consisted of twenty minutes working with my program and ten minutes of memory training. The study participants were also encouraged to spend fifteen minutes daily on pendulum ball and bean bag training, as well as memory exercises at home, and balance boards were made available to them. The control group did not receive any therapy during the same twelve-week period.

After the study, Jim and Susan compiled the data into a paper, which they presented to the International Society for Intelligence Education. The results were far more profound than I had hoped they would be. The experimental group's vision improved dramatically, including improvements in ocular motility, tracking, convergence, and peripheral vision; and there was improvement in every test of visual and auditory memory. The control group, meanwhile, showed no change over the twelve-week period.

I had anticipated the improvements in vision and visual and auditory memory, since these results were consistent with our findings at the College of Optometry and with what developmental optometrists had been seeing in their training rooms. However, the experimental group also voluntarily reported dramatic changes in numerous and diverse aspects of life. One of the participants, for example, had joined the study because she had found herself getting lost whenever she was away from home. Her husband, who was not a part of the study, had required double-bypass heart surgery, after which he had barely left the house. Their son, who worked for an airline, had offered to come and get them to take them to Europe, but they were afraid to leave their home, let alone travel abroad. The loss of mental faculty, she felt, was robbing them of what should have been the best time of their lives.

This may have been why, although some of the participants in the experimental group did not follow through on the portion of the training they were supposed to do at home, she committed herself to it. Within the first week, she began to see results. Her memory was better. Her vision was improving. She was more aware of her surroundings. It was obvious enough that something was changing that her husband started using the program as well. And by the end of the study, not only did she no longer get lost when she went out, but she and her husband were both confident enough to take their son a European vacation—and to plan to meet him in New York.

Many other participants shared improvements that, although perhaps not as dramatic, were still similar. Their driving, writing, and reading abilities had improved. They were better able to concentrate, and they retained more of the information they read. They felt more alert and more confident. They had more energy. Some said that feelings of depression had lifted. One participant even went so far as to divulge that he had become sexually active again.

Of course, this study counted as a big success for me at the time, but good feelings (and humor) aside, it also helped to shape the next phase of my thinking about the Learning Breakthrough Program.

It has been said that a problem is like the shell of an egg, with the solution always hidden inside. If that is true, then by the late 1980s, I had spent over a quarter of a century standing on top of the egg of childhood learning disabilities, trying everything from rocks to a jackhammer trying to crack it open. I woke up thinking about it. I fell asleep thinking about it. Most of my conversations had something to do with it. It was an all-consuming passion, perhaps even an obsession.

However, I wasn't actually looking at *dis*ability; I was looking at ability. The brain has a natural way of working, and what we call "disabilities" are simply impediments to that innate optimum. When we think of them, especially the ones that are most talked about—dyslexia, ADD/ADHD, and autism—because their effects are so obvious and sometimes so disastrous, we tend to think of them as "things" in and of themselves, somehow acting against the person who suffers from them.

Importantly, though, the participants in the study that Jim and Susan conducted were *becoming* less able as they got older, due to the degeneration of their sensory systems, their neural networks, and other physical structures. Before that degeneration had begun, they had been perfectly able, well-functioning individuals. The profound results that Jim and Susan had found through Learning Breakthrough activities with these individuals demonstrated that the project was not so much to chase down and conquer a disability, but to discover an ability, nurture it, and bring it to its full potential.

This idea made perfect sense in light of other observations I had made, which crystallized as I shifted my thinking from disability to ability.

Because Beverley and I ran our fledgling company out of our home, I'd had the opportunity to experience every tiny increment of our younger children's development. This had been an invaluable part of defining the program itself: because it needed to be tailored to meet the needs of the very young while also being enjoyable for teenagers and young adults, learning from our children's likes and dislikes (which they did not hesitate to share) helped to structure, refine, and instruct both the materials in the program and the activities that went along with them. Further, though, like Piaget, whose real understanding of child development came from observing what happened in his own home, I'd had the unique opportunity to watch three children develop in front of my eyes from birth.

Many of my fondest memories of the first years after moving to the Pacific Northwest are of lying on the living room floor and watching them as infants, constantly watching their environment, constantly learning from and emulating it, learning to creep, then to crawl, then to walk, and most interestingly, watching the gears turn inside their tiny heads. I am completely flabbergasted at how our culture consistently underestimates what very young children can learn and figure out for themselves. They were insatiable, determined learners, angry when they could not complete a task and full of joy when they managed to do it.

Importantly, I noticed that there was always a precursor to any new action, a phase of thought, as though they were working out the details of some new effort before they committed their bodies to movement. Sometimes, I could actually see minute movements of their muscles, which might have been spastic, or which might have been reflections of the mental process of defining their next movement.

Also, having worked with thousands of severely disorganized children in classrooms, the summer program, and at the University of Houston, I had noticed that there was a threshold of effort at which improvement in their body image began to occur rapidly. Most children with disabilities, when they first got on the balance board, had an extremely hard time keeping the board level, keeping the bean bags and ball under control, and performing the activities. Sometimes, their ability almost seemed to get worse before it got better, and in the most severe cases, it could be difficult to keep a child motivated. Trained by failure, the difficulty of the first phase of training could be so frustrating that they would want to give up. Then, after a period of work (the length of which was different for every child), the light would suddenly come on. Their body image would improve. Their movements would become more fluid. They would be more able to control the motion of a bean bag or the pendulum ball through space. And after that threshold, their improvements across the board would begin to occur at a more and more rapid pace. It's something that therapists of all kinds talk about, probably because it is the most exciting and rewarding moment in the relationship between a therapist and a patient. Up until this point, I had enjoyed the reward and I had an intuitive sense that something important was happening at that threshold, but I did not have a clear picture of what it was.

Third, in the late 80s, certain things began to change for me. I have always been an energetic person. I've always walked faster than most people, worked faster than most people, and generally lived life at a rapid, enthusiastic pace. Frustratingly, though, my body began to slow down. I needed more than five hours of sleep at night, for example. The wood and other materials that I lifted in my shop on a regular basis started to seem a little heavier. I still walked quickly, but it began to take just a little longer for me to cover the same distance.

That, of course, is natural as you get older. But I noticed something else, too, that helped me to connect the dots. At first, my mind didn't take into account the gradual slowing of the body it was attached to. My mind kept walking just as fast, lifting just as much, getting up just as early, and working just as hard. My body had trouble keeping up, but my mental body image was well established. Then, gradually, my mind began to slow down as well. For example, while still in bed in the morning, visualizing what I had to do during the day, I might imagine lifting a stack of balance boards from one table to another. Whereas before my mind would have performed this task easily, now the stack of balance boards would *feel* heavy in the mental process. I had reached a threshold at which my mind had begun to accommodate the physical changes that I was experiencing with my advancing age.

My own thinking has never gone quite as far as the mind-body philosophy, but I do know the value of visualization. Now it seemed that the mental body image plays both an instructive and a limiting role in physical ability. My young children, who all had extremely good body image as babies, had seemed to walk in their minds long before they crossed the carpet on their own feet. That mental picture had helped them to figure out what to do with each of their muscles in order to make the action happen. It had helped them. Conversely, the severely disorganized children I had worked with had had a mental body image trained by their disorganization. If a child suppressed one arm, that child didn't visualize using that arm when he imagined himself completing an activity. He left it out in the same way that I was carrying smaller stacks of balance boards in my mind. In that way, the mental image placed a limit on physical ability, thereby impeding progress.

The threshold I had observed in therapy sessions, I hypothesized, was the point at which a child's mental body image began to change. Therapy forced him, for example, to use the arm he had been leaving out, and after a period of time, that arm began showing up when he visualized an action before completing it. The mental body image, tied to the idea of a native optimum of ability, grew in importance as I considered what was really happening to create the results I had observed.

Also around this time, something else started happening. Enough time had passed since I'd started working with children that some of them had grown up. They had gotten through school. And the stories of their experience after my program began working their way through the grapevine of parent groups, therapists, counselors, and friends to our new home in the Pacific Northwest.

I will share here one personal account, which was written when I started work on this book and which is indicative of the kind of feedback I was receiving at that time.

The biggest challenge that I have overcome in my life has been learning to read. As a child, I was dyslexic. What is dyslexia? Dyslexia is a neurological disorder that creates problems with language skills. It is most often diagnosed in children after they enter school. A child will often have better than average verbal skills and intelligence. There will be no indication of a problem until the normal tasks of schoolwork are encountered.

Symptoms include the difficulty, or inability, to read past the normal age when such skills should be mastered. This neurological problem is manifested in two areas, the first being visual problems. The ability to see letters as they actually are is impaired. This is usually a directional problem, for example, b and d are often confused, as are d and p. The second area where dyslexia is manifest is in visual-motor problems. For many suffering from dyslexia, they will know the answer to the question, but will be completely unable to put that answer on paper.

My story is very typical. I had a normal intelligence level and skills when I entered Kindergarten. I could sing the ABC song with the best of them, but it became apparent I couldn't recognize any of the letters. When I wrote my name, the letters were upside down and backwards. My parents were informed that I would not be ready for first grade and would not be able to pass the basic skills tests to graduate from Kindergarten. My teacher had underestimated me though. The tests consisted of a line with a letter in the beginning and five pictures after it. The object was to circle the pictures that began with the letter identified. I had no clue what an M was, but if you showed me a mop, a mitten, a mouse, a dog, and a cat, I could tell you that the dog and the cat didn't belong. In my opinion, the M was irrelevant. In first grade, I struggled even more, I pored over "See Spot run" for hours each evening. I was furious the night I walked in and found my 2 1/2 year old brother READING my book. My parents tried to point out that he had the book upside down on his lap, and it was only that he heard me read it so many times he had it memorized, but I wasn't buying it at all.

By the end of second grade things had gone from bad to worse, I was in remedial English and Math classes, and the school wanted me to repeat the grade. My mother at this point was horrified. Her response to the school was that they didn't understand. Kids in her family usually skipped second grade, but there was no way we ever did it twice! My grandmother tried to tell her that things were just much harder for kids in our family, but fortunately, Mom never gave up. A compromise was reached, and I was allowed to enter third grade on a trial basis, if I attended a class being taught for children with learning disabilities at the University of Houston. I am probably the only 8 year old in history that has been put on academic suspension.

These classes changed my life. The instructor, Dr. Frank Belgau, had a theory that the problems children had learning to read stemmed from undeveloped connections in the brain. His concept was simple, develop those connections, and the problems would be reduced or eliminated. I spent the summer and fall that year doing simple exercises. They consisted of activities like lying on my back and doing tapping sequences with my hands and feet. In the beginning, I was unable to process these sequences. An example would be tap 3 times with your right hand, once with your right foot, 3 times with your left foot, and once with your left hand. Other activities involved standing on a balance board and throwing a bean bag up and catching it or hitting a ball suspended from the ceiling with different areas of a multicolored bat. Another important activity was to lie on my back on the floor with an orange ball suspended above me. As the ball was swung gently back and forth, I was to track its movement with my eyes, but not move my head. Prior to these exercises, when I would try to read, my eyes could not scan across a page without a glitch in the middle causing me to lose my place. By strengthening the eye muscles, that problem was corrected.

The success of this program was instantly proven. The classes began in May, and by mid-summer I was reading everything in sight. Six weeks into third grade, I was in advanced reading and math classes. I could read fluently and above grade level. More importantly, I could now put my thoughts onto paper. I finished high school with a 3.25 GPA, while still taking many college level classes in my senior year. This was significantly lower than it should have been due in large part to lack of effort, not a lack of ability. I chose not to go to college, but went to work, and raised a family. In spite of my lack of a college education, I have a very successful career. I am the Director of Investments at an independent financial services firm, and I assist in managing approximately 140 million dollars. I still like numbers a lot better than letters, but the ability to read, in vast quantities and rapidly, with a high level of comprehension, is critical to my career. The language skills needed to excel in my field are much greater than most people think. The tests required to be an investment advisor have been created by a sadistic group of people who think putting double negatives in a question is too easy to spot; they excel at writing the most convoluted ones possible. I have also obtained my CFP® passing the board exams on the first try. These exams typically have a pass rate between 53% and 62%.

The level of success I have enjoyed would have been completely impossible without overcoming the inability to read at a young age. If you investigate Dyslexia on the internet, and refer to such sites at the Mayo Clinic (www.mayoclinic.com) and Bright Solutions for Dyslexia (www.dys-add.com) you will be told that Dyslexia is incurable. I am living proof that this is not the case. I do however; harbor a deep hatred of Dick and Jane, as evidenced by my favorite T-Shirt. The front has a dog in a car and says "See Spot drive the car. Go Spot go." The back has 2 dead stick people and says "Dick and Jane didn't look both ways. Sorry Dick. Sorry Jane."

That letter has special significance to me because it was written by Jana, Beverley's daughter, the little girl who brought that beautiful walk into my program and into my life. It is also characteristic of literally hundreds of success stories. The parents of one young boy were told by a prominent child psychologist to take their son home and just love him: he would never amount to anything and shouldn't be expected to. That child completed my program at the university, and he went on to become an accomplished actor and the head of the Theater Department at Texas A&M University. Another boy, who couldn't read in his early teens because of severe dyslexia, went on to excel in school, graduate at the top of his class in college and law school, and become an extremely successful attorney, even arguing a case in front of the Supreme Court. Countless other stories were not as dramatic, but the program had a tremendous success rate.

That success rate was not 100%, and Journey Menshew's son was not one of the children who went on to have a successful life. Parents who were committed to helping their children often try more than one method; it was as true then as it is now. And in a highly acclaimed institution for the learning disabled, Journey's son was given a combination of drugs that rendered him virtually comatose. He was not alone. While one set of stories contained the thrilling implication that balance-stimulation and sensory integration had a profound effect on learning disabilities, another set of stories contained a heartbreaking human tragedy.

Brain science had still not advanced enough to provide a clear picture of why my program worked. The central piece of the whole puzzle was just beginning to receive notice, but understanding exactly how it played into the success of what I was doing was still years away. That didn't matter. From what I had observed, from the feedback I had gotten from my colleagues in Houston, from Dr. Meeker, from Dr. Schrock, and from the parents and children who had gone through my program, I knew that in a very real, practical way, my program got results.

No words can describe how it feels to help a child break through a learning disability. I have never been able to separate myself emotionally from my work or from the people I have worked with. I've always had to share their struggles with them, and sometimes it has been agonizing and frustrating to do so. But as a result I've also shared in their success.

A child picks up a book and starts reading. A child grasps the balance board and shouts, "Mommy, I can think!" A letter floats through the mail signed with a name from years ago. I can still remember the way the writer walked as a child. I can remember how he struggled to learn and the dismal future that awaited him if he couldn't. But he's a pilot now, flying some of the fastest jets in the world. She's a teacher, wanting a program for her own classroom. Or a doctor. A university professor. An athlete. A scientist. A life has changed because at some point he got up on a balance board and swung a ball over some targets or threw a bean bag up in the air and caught it.

There is no drug as addictive as seeing that change happen. There is no high as overwhelming as watching the light go on in a child's eyes and knowing that he just got it and that the world he lives in will never be the same. And, because all highs come with corollary lows, there is nothing as painful as walking through a school and seeing all the children who aren't being helped, whose light isn't coming on, who, even now, forty years after those wonderful, idealistic years in Houston, are still being warehoused in special education programs, their hands held and their futures dimmed until they turn eighteen and become somebody else's problem.

I didn't care whether I understood why my program worked. I didn't care if there hadn't been major studies done by international universities. I didn't care if I was heckled. I'd been heckled enough at the College of Optometry to grow a good, thick skin. I knew my program worked. I knew that all I had to do was get out in front of people, show them that it worked, inspire them to use it, and provide them with the Learning Breakthrough. I was in my mid-forties, and I was a junkie for changing lives.

The crusade started humbly. I still knew how to work with my hands, and we set up a shop at the house in Port Angeles to build the balance boards and other equipment that went into the Learning Breakthrough. Our first employees were our older children, who were then in high school. Beverley and I bought a big, blue Superior motor home so we could spend months at a time on the lecture circuit. (Even if gas went to a dollar a gallon, we reasoned, it would still be cheaper to drive it than to fly and pay for hotels. And when in our lifetimes was *gas* going to go to a *dollar* a gallon?)

We committed ourselves to doing whatever it took to help as many children as possible. When we started out, aside from the fact that the program worked consistently, about the only thing we had going for us was that people still paid attention to direct mail.

I was uniquely unprepared to do what I was doing. I'm not a businessman. I don't know the first thing about advertising. My reasons for leaving academia seemed valid to me, but lecturing as a young professor at a well-respected university and lecturing as an ex-academic with bold ideas are two very different things. There were still holes in my understanding; too, still missing pieces of the puzzle and, as a result, I couldn't say clearly and succinctly why my program did what it did. To say that we struggled would be a considerable understatement.

Typically, three-quarters of our audiences were teachers and therapists; the rest were parents of children with learning disabilities. Many therapists integrated the program into their therapy regimes with considerable success, and they became committed advocates. Many others saw a home-use system as a threat to clinical practice and opposed it. Teachers, too, fell into two groups, because after they had been to a lecture and seen the results, they had to go back to their schools and fight a battle against preconceived ideas in order to implement a program. Those programs were implemented here and there around the country, but more often than not, the administrative roadblocks refused to give way. Parents were more receptive, but it was often hard for a parent to take the time away from work or family to go to the lecture.

It was anything but an easy life. Beverley and I would pack our patchwork of progeny into the motor home to spend months on the lecture circuit. Then we'd go back to Port Angeles and work in the shop, making the balance boards that had been ordered. As soon as we caught up, we'd hit the road again, crisscrossing the nation like politicians in an election year. We couldn't bring ourselves to charge more than we needed to keep going, so we never made much money. Every few lectures, someone could be counted on to make a snide remark about people defying conventional wisdom. There was ridicule. There was professional snobbery. There was plenty of resistance to what we were doing.

But we kept changing lives.

And we kept on going. Through the oil embargoes of the early 1970s, as the price of gas went up. Through the end of the 70s. Through the Reagan-Bush years, through the crumbling of the Berlin Wall, through *Glasnost* and *Perestroika*. We logged more miles on that Superior motor home than it was ever intended to tally up. The road maps of the United States were seared into our minds so vividly that I can still close my eyes and trace the highways of Nebraska, Ohio, and Tennessee. We made Learning Breakthrough Program kits in batches of thirty, then fifty, then a hundred, then more than a hundred. Our shop moved out of the house and into an industrial complex in town (which made Beverley happy). The Democrats won the White House (which made our children happy). By some miracle, through it all, we managed to scrape by (which made me happy).

As the time passed, a new nucleus of minds began to form. This one was spread throughout the country, composed of teachers, therapists, and scholars from diverse backgrounds and disciplines, who were tied together by a shared dedication to helping children. There was Nancy Rowe, a speech pathologist who achieved international recognition for her ability to teach the deaf to talk and who developed a rhythm-based therapy program that has shown great promise in teaching children with autism. And Ruth Arnold, head of the Special Education department at Stetson University, who committed time, energy, and enthusiasm to the effort to define the physical roots of intelligence. Jack Harris, James Koetting, Newell Kephart, Jo Parker—with whom I had served on the committee that drafted the nation's first formal law dealing with learning disabilities—Jerry Winger, Mary Meeker, Ralph Schrock, and many others whose lives and work had crossed mine over the years, formed ad hoc working groups and wrote endless letters, striving closer and closer to understanding what was really at the heart of the work we were doing.

And science continued its inexorable march toward understanding. Brain mapping began and evolved by leaps and bounds. Researchers at universities in the United States, in Europe, and elsewhere drew an increasingly clear picture of how the internal processes of the brain interact with the outside world, how the marvels of our ability are made possible, and how the neurons actually work. Through it all, a faculty of the brain that had been talked about in the 1970s, but which had never really been understood, started coming to the fore: the vestibular system.

As it was defined, we understood why the activities we were doing were so effective. They weren't just changing body image. They were changing the brain.

Chapter 25:

THE MISSING LINK

Our understanding of how the brain operates is constantly changing. Its mechanics are a new frontier, to which science is giving increasing attention, and as the sharp minds in today's laboratories cut deeper into the tissue of that organ, new discoveries will shed new light, new understanding will lead to new insights, and what we know today will seem primitive only a few years in the future.

As you read this explanation, it is important to keep that in mind. This is only one explanation, and although it is based on what I have observed and on the best of what we know, I'm sure it will be shaped by new knowledge. I comfort myself that I am not alone in postulating from the known into the unknown. Some of the leading medical establishments in the world still say dyslexia is incurable and yet, forty years ago, the program I developed corrected the underlying cause of Jana's dyslexia. For years, the leading treatment of ADD/ADHD was to give children amphetamines, a band-aid solution that is now proving to have severe side effects. I may not be one hundred percent correct, but at least I believe my ideas are more correct than those!

This understanding evolved slowly, through my experience with thousands of children, through my interaction with some of the best minds in education and child development, and through the natural refining process that comes from lecturing and having to answer the often probing questions from my audiences. Forty-five years ago, when I went blustering into F. E. McGahan's office and told him that "Organizing three-dimensional space, time, and energy must be a fundamental component of human intelligence," I was taking a shot in the dark. Call it beginner's luck, but I was on to something. And over the years, the discoveries made by the scientific community and my own observations have put a great deal of flesh on those bones.

Chapter 26:

NEURAL NETWORKS AND
NEURAL PLASTICITY

The basic unit of the human nervous system, including the brain, the spinal column, and the nerves, is the "neuron." A neuron typically consists of a cell body, which contains a nucleus and receives incoming nerve impulses, and an axon, which carries nerve impulses away. A single neuron, however, is incapable of any order; it fires at random. Neurons only become organized en masse, and it takes a tremendous number of neurons—millions even for a simple action—for the brain to react. As a task gets more difficult, the number of neurons required to accomplish it increases exponentially, and the efficiency with which the neurons fire defines the efficiency of your reaction to a stimulus.

A neural network is the human body's marvelous method of increasing the efficiency of neurological activity. The neuron senses the nerve impulse in its membrane, and it "fires" an impulse through its axon. This excites other neurons, which also fire. Over time, through repetitions of an activity, certain neurons become connected, through axons, creating a network of neurons that are hyper-responsive to each other. The configuration of that network defines the action it is established to accomplish; and when neurons within the network receive an impulse, the whole network fires. The more a network is used, the stronger the connections between neurons become, increasing the efficiency and functioning of the network.

Take, for example, the act of throwing a ball and hitting a target. When you first pick up a ball and throw it, your aim isn't good; you can't throw it with much velocity. You're a long way away from trying out for the Yankees. This is because the neurons in your brain aren't organized into an efficient network to accomplish that task. Other networks that approximate the action are being used instead: for instance, if you chop wood before you throw a ball for the first time, your muscles and the neural configuration for chopping wood might approximate the action required to throw a ball. However, the more you practice, the more the neural network needed for the specific action of throwing a ball develops and strengthens. Given enough time and enough practice, you just might end up with a network efficient enough and an action precise enough to go out for the Yankees.

Neurons can be a part of more than one neural network, hence participating in literally hundreds of actions. Parts of one neural network can be incorporated into another, refining learned actions to be applied to new circumstances. And your nervous system contains billions of neurons. This creates an incredible potential for creating new neural networks, for adaptation of old ones—for learning new tricks whether you are young or old. This potential is called neural plasticity: the ability of the brain to produce neurons and to develop new neural networks throughout its life. Neural plasticity is most commonly discussed in reference to recovery from brain damage, as it is the process that allows new networks to be developed in an undamaged portion of the brain to replace those lost in a damaged portion of the brain.

Neural plasticity, and the development of neural networks, are also fundamental to the development of the brain in its earliest stages.

Chapter 27:

MAKING SENSE: THE BEGINNING

As a fetus matures in the womb, the first sense to develop and to begin sending information to the central nervous system is the vestibular sense. This sense consists of two symmetrical physical structures, located in the inner ear on each side of the child's head. Each inner ear is made up of three semicircular canals, partially filled with fluid, and an organ called the otolyth.

The three semicircular canals are positioned in such a way that they measure motion along three planes: pitch, or forward-backward motion; roll, or left-to-right motion; and yaw, or the motion of tilting from side to side. The speed and degree of motion is measured by the behavior of the fluid within those semicircular canals. As the fluid moves over delicate, tiny hairs, those hairs move; very sensitive nerve cells at the base of the hairs detect their movement, registering the velocity and direction of the fluid in the canals.

The simplest way to get a visual picture of this is to run some water into a glass and move it around. The water in the glass responds to gravity, and you can see how far and how quickly you tip the glass by how the water inside it behaves. Obviously, the inner ear is more sophisticated, but fluid in any vessel responds the same way. Importantly, the fluid has two reference points: inertia and the force of gravity.

The otolyth is composed of two parts: the utricle and the saccule. The utricle is composed of calcium carbonate crystals, embedded in a pendulum-like membrane. This pendulum senses the force and direction of motion in reference to the always-vertical force of gravity, providing the brain with a precise and reliable gauge of three-dimensional motion. The saccule is an internal detector similar to the semicircular canals. A small sac partially filled with fluid, it detects and measures the vertical motion of the head in three-dimensional space. (If you cover the top of your glass of water and move it up and down, you can visualize an approximation of how the saccule gets its measurements.)

The vestibular system is very sensitive, and it provides the developing brain with information relative to any movement of the head through three-dimensional space. Because an identical inner ear apparatus is located on each side of the head, the central nervous system gathers this information in stereo, providing for higher resolution, and defines a three-dimensional inertial space referenced to gravity. This structure is vital, not only for the developing fetus, but for a full-grown person as well: every spatial conception, from the internal sense of your own body, the relative position of each of your own body parts, and the direction and speed of each part's motion through three-dimensional space, depends on this phenomenon.

And remember: this is the first sense that develops in the womb. For a developing organism that has not yet gained the capacity to see, to hear, to activate movement, or to feel, this sense provides the first sense of relationship with the world. Neural networks, the fundamental structures of brain processing, form to handle the information derived by this sensory structure: they are the first sensory networks to form in the developing brain, and they become the template for the development of other neural networks.

As the vestibular system develops and senses motion, the process of sensing helps to stimulate the growth of the nerves that connect to its various physical structures. When muscles begin to develop, they are not controlled by a highly organized brain, which tells them what to do. Their first movements are reflex movements, caused by disorganized impulses. But those spastic or reflex movements are the first source of self-initiated movement for the fetus. The vestibular system senses these movements, and, like any physical structure, with exercise, it grows more robust. Those movements also stimulate the pressure and motion detectors in the muscles and joints of the body and the tactile detectors on the skin of the body, face, ears, and lips. These detectors excite the central nervous system: it is the first experience with sensation, causing a swell of neurological activity.

At this early stage of development, the vestibular system is the only developed sensory apparatus, meaning that the neural networks attached to it are the only developed sensory networks. One of the great mysteries—and also one of the great miracles—of how the brain works is that neural networks are shared, based on relevance to prior stimuli.

One way to understand this is through the metaphor of cooking. The more cooking you do, the more recipes you know. Those recipes can be equated to neural networks. When you come across a new ingredient, you don't just start learning to cook again from scratch: you immediately begin to work that ingredient into the recipes you already know. Eventually, you might create a whole new recipe surrounding this ingredient, but that happens later. In the same way, when we are exposed to a new stimulus or a new action, we initially use already-established neural networks to deal with it.

Most likely, then, when the fetus first experiences the wave of new sensory information coming from the muscles and the skin, the neural networks developed for the vestibular system are first in line to make sense of it. The direction of the body movement relative to gravity and the direction of the flow of amniotic fluid over the skin are matched with the direction and velocity of the rate of flow of the more highly developed vestibular structures, and the first multisensory awareness of the body moving through space comes into focus. Gradually, over time, new neural networks develop to handle the subtlety of different kinds of stimuli. The motor sense (muscle-driven movement of the body) and the sense of touch develop their own neurological structures, but those structures remain fundamentally connected to, and influenced by, the vestibular sense.

At this point in the life of a developing fetus, the brain is doing at a lower resolution exactly what a student does in a classroom, exactly what a scientist does in a laboratory. In a rudimentary fashion, with newly formed tools, the brain is making sense of information.

Developing Senses, Developing Sense

As a fetus grows in size and sophistication in the womb, the other senses develop in much the same way.

Six muscles, called extraocular muscles, develop around each eye. By twenty weeks after conception, the motor system of these muscles reaches a point at which, when the head and body move, the eyes are held stable relative to the three-dimensional world. There is no way for the eyes to "know" what level is except for the information sensed by the vestibular system. In fact, these extraocular muscles work in oppositional pairs. One pair in each eye is connected to one semicircular canal. As the fluid moves through that semicircular canal, the sense of motion instructs the muscles of the eye how to respond to counterbalance the movement of the body through space.

Also by twenty weeks, the ears and the audio sensory system have developed. The child hears the beat of its mother's heart, but that sound is not constant. As it moves inside the womb, closer to or further away from the mother's heart, the intensity of the sound changes. As it turns, the direction of the sound changes. These changes are also referenced to information from the vestibular system. The vestibular system constantly measures movement; the intensity of the sound changes relative to that movement; and from that correlation, the child begins to establish an awareness of three-dimensional auditory space.

It is important to recognize that these sensory systems do not develop independently. As each new sensory apparatus grows, the brain initially processes the information that comes from it using existing neural networks. Neural networks dedicated to each sense develop over time as the sensory apparatus becomes more distinct, but they retain a high level of interconnection. They also have a natural tendency to entrain, or work together. That is to say, information often comes to the brain from more than one sense; multiple senses gather the information, compare it, and develop a higher-resolution picture than would come from any single sense by itself.

Each new sense that develops provides the fetal brain with another source of information in its never-ending quest to make sense of its environment. In the protected environment of the womb, it makes sense only of the physical information coming to it from its rapidly developing vestibular, motor, tactile, and auditory senses. But the fundamental processes—the integration of information sources, the neural networks, and the reference to inertia and gravity—provide the foundation of everything the child will experience after birth.

A Child Meets the World

When a child enters the world, she has already developed a rudimentary but still remarkable concept of three-dimensional space. From the tactile sense, she knows where her body ends and the rest of the universe begins.

She has a rudimentary sense of auditory space, based on movement and hearing inside the womb. She has enough experience with her motor sense to know when she is the one initiating a movement and when the movement is being initiated by a caregiver. When she opens her eyes and begins to use them to see the three-dimensional space around her, and the objects in that space, she begins to make sense of her visual world.

At this time, the most developed of the senses, and the one that experiences the least transition between the environment inside the womb and the environment outside, is the vestibular sense. As the newborn baby begins to experience the world and its great abundance of new sensations, as she begins to explore that world and the way her body works in that world, the vestibular system once again operates as a cornerstone and catalyst of her ability to make sense of her surroundings.

She has also been learning while inside the womb. The birth of our youngest daughter, Beth, was not an easy one. It was a natural childbirth; Beverley wasn't on anything for pain; and the pain she was going through and the physical difficulty of the birth were both excruciating.

Dr. Roger Oaks, who was delivering the baby, created, in contrast, an extremely peaceful environment. He was polished and professional. He was positive and encouraging. Even though it was a painful delivery for both Beverley and Beth, his presence permeated the room with a sense of security that filled what might have been a divisive room with a sense of gratitude. As a result, both Beverley and I kept our heads.

Throughout her pregnancy, Beverley had sung *Edelweiss* to Beth. We knew that although our children couldn't understand the words we were saying while they were in the womb, their auditory sense had formed and they could *hear* us. So we always made it a point to talk to them, sing to them, and call them by name before they were born. Beth's song had been *Edelweiss*.

So after that difficult birth, when Dr. Oaks handed Beth, brand-spanking new, to Beverley, she sang *Edelweiss*. Beth had endured a trying experience, too. Being born into the world is hard enough; when extra pain and tension are added to that, the trauma is even greater, and you could see it on her face. But as soon as the song began, she opened her eyes wide and looked at Beverley with a sense of wonder. She recognized the tune.

And then, all of a sudden, she started to move her arms like a music conductor, waving them back and forth in arcs in time to the music. Her arms didn't make spastic jerks: it was a refined, smooth, rhythmic motor structure. At the moment of her birth, she was already able to hear a tune (a sensory function), to recognize it (a cognitive function), and to move her arms in time with it (a three-dimensional motor function). An *underlying structure* had already been built in her brain.

Anybody who has had or worked with newborns knows that unless they need food, a diaper change, or someone to hold them, they are very receptive, observant little creatures. When their mother speaks or sings, they turn their head toward her. They look. They listen. When someone holds out a finger, they grasp it and hold it. When objects move in close proximity, they watch them. When music plays, they often move along with it. They move—sometimes, it seems, just to feel themselves move. Later, when they escape the confines of arms and baby rockers and begin to creep, crawl, and walk, they tend to explore their world with curiosity, innocence, and zeal.

During this period, the senses that developed inside the womb are coming into focus, and once again the infant experiences a surge of stimulation—and develops new processes to handle the extra information. Although these new processes probably won't last, she is beginning to remember: she knows the members of her immediate family; she knows the people who are in her environment on a regular basis; and she knows when a stranger appears. She knows when she needs something: when she's hungry, when she feels alone, when her diaper makes her uncomfortable. She learns that when she cries, she gets the attention she needs.

Every time I watch a baby begin to interact with her world, I'm struck by the miracle of it. It seems impossible: day after day she strides ahead, growing in her understanding, in her awareness, in her ability to provoke action. She cries. Then she coos. Then she babbles. One day, she speaks. She moves in place. Then she rolls over. Then she creeps. Then she crawls. And then, one day, she walks. In the time it has taken to write this book, a baby will go from being lost and dependent in a brand new world to being a toddler with likes, dislikes, needs, wants, preferences, and sibling rivalries. It is so profound and so magical to watch that it almost defies understanding.

That rapid rate of development is possible because of the integrated network of senses that she has already established when she is born. It might be a stretch to say that Beth was using language when she waved her arms in time to *Edelweiss*; but she was using the same *processes* that define language. I see a tree (a sensory function), I recognize it (a cognitive function), and I react to it by saying the word "tree" (a three-dimensional motor function). I've now developed a mental library of words and linguistic systems, so I can put my communication into the form of advanced language, but I still use the same organizational structure.

That structure allows the child to organize the chaos of stimulation she experiences when she enters the world. It allows her to make sense of them, to learn to contend with them, and to develop all the abilities that make her so cute and hard to say "no" to when she's young.

Once again, new kinds of information are processed by existing neural networks. Over time, they develop their own neural networks. Still, her vestibular system is the most developed; it is still the template for new neurological structures; and because the child's position in reference to gravity is so fundamental to her development, the vestibular sense is still highly involved in the continuing development of her brain.

Chapter 28:

THE "HIGHER" BRAIN

Even though the structure is in place, the brain doesn't come out of the box fully formed. The *potential* for its formation exists, but it develops and changes based on our need to interact with our environment. Any time we learn to do something new, any time we're confronted by a stimulus we haven't experienced before, any time our environment demands that we adapt, our brain develops further.

This is true whether we're learning to throw a ball or learning to read. New neural networks form; new sensory and processing apparatus evolve. The higher brain, home of all the human traits that are so mystifying, has its roots firmly planted in the parts of the brain that allow us to sense the world around us, which have their roots firmly planted in the vestibular system.

This is why activities that promote balance and spatial awareness have such a profound effect on "higher" brain functions like reading, memory, and evaluation. We all have native inefficiencies in our vestibular system. Our lifestyles contribute to those inefficiencies, and certain lifestyles (like sitting in front of a computer all day) can add new ones. Those inefficiencies exist at the root of our brain's function. Through that highly integrated system of neural processing with which we make sense of our world, those inefficiencies repeat and repeat, impeding the efficiency of every facet of our intellectual life.

When you do activities that increase the efficiency of the vestibular-based multisensory framework, you increase the efficiency of your whole brain.

The Multi-Sensory Operating Space

The basic edict of the human brain within a physical environment is to orient the body within that environment and to enable it to move safely and effectively through it. To do this, we create a multi-sensory operating space, essentially, our experiential version of the world around us. The interaction with this operating space is what I observed when I watched the infinitesimal increments of my own children's development, when I brought severely disorganized children across the threshold at which rapid improvement began, and when I noticed the change in my own mental body image as I confronted the physical limitations of advancing age.

The multi-sensory operating space is the sum of a number of constituent parts. To fully understand this complex, multi-factored phenomenon, we must study each of the parts—sensing or otherwise gathering raw data, measuring this data, categorizing and sorting the data, and establishing relationships with past experiences to give meaning to the data—within the context of the whole. Each stage of the process is important. An inefficiency at any stage results in lower-resolution perception. The lower the resolution of our multi-sensory operating space, the less able we are to successfully operate within our environment.

Gathering Data

At all times, the body is collecting masses of data. Some of it is processed consciously; the vast majority is simply taken in and filed away. Our ability to collect this data has a direct impact on our ability to survive: if you cannot sense your environment, you cannot operate within it.

To get a picture of this, imagine that you are reading this book on an airplane, on your way to a ten-day vacation in Hawaii.

Let's say you're flying economy, sitting in seat 17C, on the aisle right around the middle of the airplane. To your left is a handsome businessman wearing too much cologne. To your right, across the aisle, is a young child. The movie is a romantic comedy, but you don't care what the title is. You're busy reading this!

Meanwhile, your body is busy collecting information. Your sense of sight is delivering the verbal information from the page. In your periphery, you are also keeping track of the movements of the child to your right and, perhaps, of the businessman to your left. Vaguely, you are noticing the flicker of the video screens. You are monitoring any changes in light. And so on.

Your sense of touch is in a heightened state of alert because of the anxiety associated with flying. Even if you're a member of the million-mile club, you still know intuitively that you're thirty thousand feet up; even if you've downed a couple cocktails so you won't be quite so aware, your body is still paying close attention to the airplane to make sure everything is going smoothly. Every minute vibration of the plane, every hiccup of turbulence, every breath of air across your skin—everything—is being gathered with extra sensitivity.

Your sense of hearing, too, is acutely alert, capturing every sound the plane makes, as well the sounds of the child sitting to your right, who has just started playing a hand-held video game that keeps beeping, the white noise of conversations all around you, and the occasional announcements coming from the flight attendants and the pilot.

Your sense of taste is working, detecting the slightly salty residue of the peanuts you ate just after takeoff, mixed with the tangy sweetness of ginger ale, or perhaps the cocktails you drank so you wouldn't be anxious about flying.

Your sense of smell is taking in the scent of the handsome businessman's cologne, the scent of the meal cart as it trundles down the aisle, the scent of processed air that always fills an airplane cabin, and the various scents of the other passengers.

You also sense all of your body's internal signals. You are hungry, and the nagging desire for food is persistent. You are a little tired. Although you've only been in the air for a couple of hours, your legs ache from the small, economy seats with too little legroom. The week preceding your vacation was especially busy, and there is a lingering tension in your neck.

And your sense of balance, or vestibular sense, is constantly monitoring the position of your head and body in space, maintaining your posture for comfort while you read. It is sensing how level the plane is, whether it is climbing or descending, whether it tilts to the left or right, and so on.

Your brain collects all this information. But what does it do with it? Why is it that, with all this going on, you are still able to focus on the book?

Measuring Data

All of the data that your senses collect must be measured and assessed in order to be relevant. In order to do this, you have established your own tolerance levels for various phenomena, and those tolerance levels act as a reference from which to measure each piece of data.

For example, if you are extremely sensitive to the scent of certain colognes, and if the businessman to your left happens to be wearing a cologne to which you are sensitive, then the scent of his cologne might exceed your tolerance level. It might be difficult to ignore; it might make you feel nauseated; you might have to see if you can change seats in order to get away from it.

The same goes for the beeping of that handheld video game that the childboy to your right is playing. If you are overly sensitive to certain sounds, the video game might exceed your tolerance level. It might just be a little bit irritating. Or it might be distracting enough that you would to ask the child to stop playing the game or put in earplugs to block out the sound.

Also, you have a sense of what constitutes the normal workings of an airplane. There is, of course, some level of vibration. Certain sounds, like the movement of wing flaps or the popping open of wheel wells, are well within those normal parameters. If you are afraid of flying, those parameters might be narrower. If you are extremely comfortable—or drunk from those pre-flight cocktails—the parameters might be broader. Everything you sense from the airplane itself is measured against those parameters.

Aside from the natural tendency to let your attention roam a little, you only become consciously aware of sensory data when it crosses the tolerance threshold you have established in your mind, because that is the base point for your sensory measuring stick.

Categorizing and Sorting Data

Regardless of whether a piece of data crosses your tolerance threshold, it must be sorted and categorized once it has been collected. This is an essential part of the process of creating an operational facsimile of your physical environment: essentially, as you sort and categorize data, you are constructing the world around you, moment by moment, with the building blocks of sensory data.

For example, you sort data by intensity. Under smell, you might have "cologne" at the top of the list, followed by "food," followed by "processed air." Under sound, you might have "that bleeping beeping," followed by "airplane sounds," followed by "conversation noise."

Also, you sort by importance. If you are highly anxious about flying, all the data pertaining to the plane will have an extra importance. If you are extremely hungry, the smell of food might trump the businessman's cologne.

As well as sorting it, you categorize the data, and this enables you to cross-reference data collected from various senses in order to create a multi-sensory, multi-dimensional operating space. You may, for example, catch a distant whiff of the scent of rubber that is nowhere near an intensity that would cross your tolerance threshold. Your feet may feel a slight change in vibration, but nothing too far out of the ordinary. You might hear a slight agitation in the sound of a wing flap moving. Taken independently, each of these sensory data would not arouse suspicion. Cross-referenced, however, they would combine to alert you to a potential problem with the plane, and a potential threat to your safety.

It is important to recognize that the senses support each other and that the integration of the senses is necessary in order to create an accurate mental picture of the world.

Putting the Data in Context

Now the data has been gathered. It has been measured, sorted, and categorized. You have in your mind a moment-by-moment facsimile of the world around you, a multi-sensory, multi-dimensional operating space. So what?

Without being put in context, none of the data means anything. Even as I was describing these processes, I could not *describe* the data without attaching meaning to it. The context into which you fit the data that you gather consists of *everything* you have learned. Every moment since conception, you have gathered data; every stimulus to which you have reacted has taught you something about similar stimuli; and the sum total of all that experience gives everything within your operating space meaning.

How much turbulence can a plane handle? What does normal engine noise sound like? What do you think of handsome businessmen? What about handsome businessmen who wear too much cologne? Is it acceptable for a child to play with a noisy video game on the plane? Do you like airplane food? How much room do you need for your legs to be comfortable? And so on.

The Dynamics of an Operating Space.

Now let's look at the creation of a multi-sensory operating space in greater depth. Fundamentally, any system that converts raw data into meaningful information must contain a system for collecting data, a system for measuring data, a system for sorting and categorizing data, and a system for putting data in context.

For maximum efficiency, each phase of this process must be matched appropriately with all other phases in the process. A highly efficient data collection system, coupled with a mediocre measuring system, will produce a mediocre operating space. A mediocre collecting system coupled with a highly efficient measuring system will also produce only a mediocre operating space. The resolution of your operating space is dependent upon the efficiency of each element.

Historically, in trying to determine the basis of sensation and perception, each sensory modality has been studied as a separate entity and looked upon as an independent system. Vision is vision. Hearing is hearing. Touch is touch. But each of these senses only *contributes* to the creation of an operating space, and they are necessary only insofar as they contribute to that operating space. They are part of a larger system.

To understand this clearly, let's say, for example, that while you are sitting on the airplane, you *feel* a sudden gust of air from behind you. You *hear* a loud rushing sound. You *turn* around, surprised, to *see* what has happened.

Take a moment to look at the following diagram.

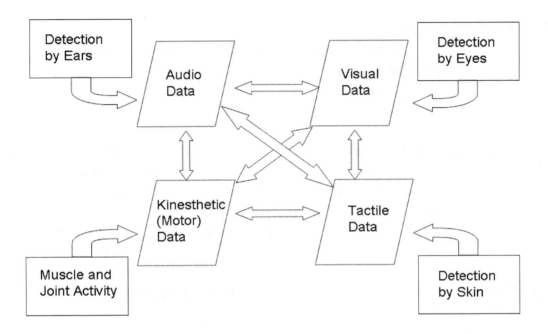

Fig. 1. Creating an operating space involves many processes and streams of data.

This simple schematic illustrates the integration of the sensory systems you just used to establish that the passenger sitting behind you, in turning on the fan over his seat, accidentally turned it on when it was aimed at your head. The tactile information from your skin first alerted you that something was wrong. You located the source of the disturbance by hearing the rushing sound and placing it within the threedimensional space around you. That told your body where to turn; your kinesthetic. or motor, sense measured and monitored the turning of your head, and your eyes picked out the offending overhead fan.

To gain an even greater appreciation of how important the integration of the senses are, perform the following experiments. (If you are actually on an airplane flying to Hawaii, you might wait until you reach your hotel room. You might wake up the handsome businessman or interrupt other passengers, if the act of performing these experiments crosses their sensory threshold.)

Experiment 1: Multi-Sensory Data Gathering

Required materials:
- audio recording device (e.g., a personal tape recorder or dictating machine)
- reading material

Process
1. From your reading material, read aloud a couple of paragraphs—as much as a page—using your tape recorder to record your reading. Be sure to speak clearly as you read aloud.
2. Replay, at twice the recorded speed, the material you just read aloud. Do not reference your reading material. Listen carefully to the recording and try to make out what is being said.
3. Again, replay the sequence at twice the recorded speed. This time, read along with the recording, using your reading material. Again, try to make out what is being said.

Discussion

Did you notice that, when you first listened to the material at double speed, you could not make sense out of what you were hearing? Did you then notice that, when you played the recording at double speed and read along in your reading material, you were able to actually hear the words you were reading?

This experiment illustrates not only that the senses are connected and that sensory information gathered by one sense supports the information connected by another sense, but also that the development of a multi-sensory operating space, and our ability to make sense of that operating space, *depends* upon input from all our senses.

To take the experiment a step further, try memorizing a few sentences of the reading material and then playing the recorded reading of that same material at double speed. Of course, once you have memorized the material, you will be even more able to *hear* what is being played on the recording because the material will already be part of the context of your operating space. You will recognize information that has previously been sorted and categorized, and that information will feed your sensory awareness, increasing the resolution of your operating space.

Experiment 2: Impact of Auditory Stimulus

Required materials:
- audio playing device
- tape, CD, or MP3 with repetitive rhythm

Process
1. Stand with your feet together and bounce up and down to a rhythm that you create internally.
2. Play the tape, CD, or MP3 with a repetitive beat. You will naturally begin to move with that rhythm.
3. After you have established that rhythm and are moving up and down to it comfortably, stop the audio.
4. Continue to bounce to the rhythm that was on the audio, now that it is no longer playing.

Discussion
Did you notice that, once you were bouncing up and down to your internal rhythm, you could "hear" that rhythm in your head? Did you notice that, as soon as the external rhythm began from the audio, it became uncomfortable to continue to move to your internal rhythm? Did you notice that, when you then removed the audio stimulation, it became more difficult to maintain the rhythm that it had provided?

Initially, when you moved to your internal rhythm, you were using already stored sensory information to create a sensory experience in your mind. That rhythm came from somewhere. It was something you heard and remembered from some experience earlier in your life, either from some other audio experience or from the natural rhythms of your own body, (e.g., your heartbeat). At that point in the experiment, you were creating an element in your internal auditory space that did not exist in your physical environment.

As soon as you turned on the audio source, if the external rhythm clashed with your internal rhythm, dissonance was created between your operating space and your sensory experience. As soon as you began to move with the rhythm supplied by the audio recording, your movements became more natural, and the act of moving with the beat required less energy than it had before the audio recording began.

Simply put, in the first scenario, *you* were creating a rhythm; you were providing that rhythm to your body and thinking about your movements in order to make them match that rhythm. When you added the audio and entrained to the rhythm provided by your senses, the movement became automatic: the external rhythm provided the order, or structure, to guide the movements of your body. When you move, neurons fire in your brain. But not all neurons in a neural network fire at the same time. Some fire early, some fire on time, and some fire late: the relative efficiency of your movement depends on the percentage of neurons firing on time. When you added the recorded auditory signal, more neurons fired together. Hearing the sound radiated throughout the multi-sensory structure. The motor neurons entrained to the rhythm and fired in a more synchronized manner because the added sensory input increased the neural efficiency of your response.

Then, when you stopped playing the audio recording, you again required more energy to move. At this point, you were recalling the sensory experience, applying it to create an auditory component of your operating space, and moving to that rhythm.

You can try this experiment using different senses as well. If you stand opposite another person who is also bouncing to an internal rhythm, you will both naturally entrain to a single rhythm and, guided by sensory (visual) input, you will expend less energy moving to that rhythm than to separate ones. If you hold an object in your hand that pulses to a rhythm, you will entrain to that rhythm, and, again, when your motion and sensory experience are in time, it will require less energy to move.

Additionally, if you were to hold a pulsing object in your hand, listen to a rhythm from an audio source, *and* watch another person move, all to the same rhythm, the input from multiple senses would support your movement even more, and it would require even less energy. If you held the pulsing object, listened to a rhythm from an audio source, and watched another person moving, all to the same rhythm, and you tried to move to a different rhythm, you would expend extra energy to maintain your focus and to overcome the sensory input from your physical environment. If you held the pulsing object, listened to an audio rhythm, and watched someone moving, all to different beats, you would have a difficult time finding any individual rhythm to follow because the dissonance of the sensory input would impede your ability to entrain.

Experiment 3: Impact of Visual Stimulus on Physical Balance

Process

1. Stand on both feet. Keep your body still and balanced. Then stand on one foot and continue to keep your body still and balanced. Then stand on the other foot and continue to keep your body still and balanced.
2. Close your eyes.
3. Stand on both feet with your eyes closed. Then stand on one foot with your eyes closed. Then stand on the other foot with your eyes closed.
4. Now stand on both feet, then one foot, and then the other foot, with your eyes closed the entire time. When you feel yourself losing balance, open your eyes to steady yourself.

Discussion

Did you notice that, when you closed your eyes, it was more difficult to maintain your balance? Did you notice that, when you were balancing with your eyes closed, lost balance, and opened your eyes, it was easier to correct yourself? Did you notice, also, that it was easier to maintain your sense of balance on one foot than it was on the other?

This experiment speaks for itself. The difference in your ability to balance when your eyes are open versus when they are closed is indicative of a high level of integration between your visual system and your motor system.

It also demonstrates that the level of integration between the visual and motor senses is relative to balance, and that this integration becomes more important as the effort required to maintain balance is increased. The visual input was not as important when you were standing more stably on both feet. It became more important when you were standing on one foot and were, consequently, less stable.

In this case, the visual system supported the motor system and your sense of balance. Receiving input from multiple sensory systems created a higher-resolution operating space, and you were more capable of orienting yourself within it. It also took less energy to maintain your balance with the visual input than it did without that input.

If you were to visualize, in perfect detail with your eyes closed, the room in which you are now sitting, the visualized image of the room, although created by your mind instead of your sensory systems, would also support the motor and balance senses and make it easier for you to maintain your balance. The level to which this visualization would support the other senses would depend upon its resolution: the better your ability to access the data you have stored, the higher the resolution of your operating space, and the more able you are to orient yourself and operate within an environment.

Chapter 29:

THE BRAIN IN A CLASSROOM

We often think of the brain as a magical entity that somehow absorbs information, and this may be the greatest failure of the education system: we put all our energy into determining *what* information should be absorbed and in *what order* it should be absorbed, but we don't pay nearly enough attention to *how* that magic works.

What is the information that a student in a classroom—or anybody in any environment, for that matter—absorbs? It is sensory stimulation, processed and made sensible by an intricately integrated brain.

One of the great complexities of understanding what was actually happening in the brain based on external observations of children is that, from an external point of view, it appears that the brain is using one process at a time. When you hear, for example, it is natural to observe that your auditory sense is working. In reality, though, sensory processing, making sense of sensory stimulation, and reacting to it is a whole brain activity. Rather than one process occurring at a time, it is as though a symphony is playing together and, for a moment, one member of the symphony plays a little louder. At all times, however, numerous underlying processes are contributing to every action.

The words on a page come to the mind through the eyes, which move across the page and stay level and focused as they read them. Each phoneme is a three-dimensional object: for the lips, the tongue, the vocal chords, and the jaw, it has a shape, without which it is meaningless. The words themselves relate to the three-dimensional world: the internal picture that manifests in a student's mind derives partly from the words on the page and partly from the multisensory operating space that the student has already established.

The same is true of mathematics. At its essence, math is a numerical representation of the world. It is a description. It is, unto itself, an operating space. And a student's ability to realize that space, to understand the relationships within it and the rules that define it, whether the subject is basic arithmetic or advanced quantum physics, depends on the resolution of the sensual operating space.

The physical universe exists within the academic universe. It is its foundation; it is what gives the academic universe meaning; intellectual inquiry is a process of gaining understanding of that physical universe, of its dimensions and its implications, of its history, and of our place within it. And physical intelligence, which has its root in the resolution of the relationship between the body and the forces of gravity and inertia (which are sensed by the vestibular system), exists profoundly in academic intelligence.

The brain's process of development, which begins in the womb and continues into adulthood, provides the foundation of learning. An individual's abilities derive from the efficiency of those systems, from the basic organization that manifests itself through the integrated coils of evolving, expanding neurological systems. Disabilities derive from an inefficiency in that basic organization, repeated and repeated like the reflections in a hall of mirrors, hampering the efficiency even of seemingly unrelated regions of the brain.

The manifestations of those inefficiencies can be diverse. The students I worked with in the classrooms in Houston, in the Perceptual Motor and Visual Perception Lab, and in the various environments I experienced later in life had a wide variety of learning disabilities. Some were dyslexic. Some had auditory processing disorders. Some had attention deficit disorders. Some fell somewhere on the autism spectrum. Some had Down Syndrome. No two children were the same. Some suffered from severe disabilities that rendered them incapable of even the simplest tasks. Some had minor disabilities; they were still able to learn; they just couldn't learn as well as would be indicated by their intelligence.

But almost all of these children responded to the same activities. I didn't need to invent one program for dyslexic children, another program for children with attention deficit disorders, and yet another for children with auditory processing disorders. I needed only to refine the highly integrated commonality of senses, including audio, visual, tactile, and motor processing, built upon that most basic of sensory structures, the vestibular sense. I had only to redefine the child's relationship with the forces of gravity and inertia.

In the same way that an inefficiency reflects and reflects through that hall of mirrors, the solution, magically, reflects and reflects as well. The body has a marvelous potential for adaptation; the brain has an inherent attraction toward order. When we corrected, admittedly by strokes of luck, the fundamental inefficiencies from which those students' disabilities had evolved, we solved the disabilities as well.

And with that, the code was cracked. It made sense.

Chapter 30:

THE CRUSADE CONTINUES

Crusades are interesting things. They change over the years. They begin with a fever of passion and recklessness. They drive you to pursue courses of action that are both wise, like continuing to work with children, and foolish, like leaving academia in disgust. Most importantly, the beginning of a crusade is defined by the question, which echoes in your mind like a shout: "What can I do?" And whatever the answer is, you go out and do it.

Real passion never cools; it has its own rewards, quite different from the comparatively shallow ends of wealth and esteem; but it does change as you grow older and as your perspective changes. One person, two people, even a small and committed community of people, can accomplish only so much in their lifetimes. At a certain point, the wise crusader must acknowledge that the question echoing in his ears is no longer, "What can I do?" but "What can be done?"

I have spent nearly a lifetime working with learning-disabled children, and it has been a labor of love second to none I can imagine. Years ago, George Phillips told me that the purpose of an airplane was to fly. My purpose in life was to teach these kids. And like an airplane skirting clouds and glittering in the sun, I was happiest when I was with them, laughing and working and struggling and learning as they did.

But for all my affection for those children, I also know they are a burden on society. Individuals with learning disabilities are far more likely to fail in school. They are far more likely to reject social rules and conventions, to be disruptive in classrooms, to start fights, to use drugs and alcohol, to participate in crime, to require public assistance, to spend time in jail, to be abusive to their spouses and their children, and by so doing, to perpetuate cycles of violence into future generations.

The largest industry in the United States today is the prison system. Although statistics vary, and although their validity is questionable in some cases, it is fair to say that, the vast majority of inmates in our prisons suffer from a learning disability. In schools, learning-disabled children require their own classrooms and their own instructors. The special education department in public schools carries the highest per capita cost of any department. Social services such as welfare and subsidized drug rehabilitation cost the government and taxpayers billions of dollars each year, and a disproportionate percentage of recipients are individuals with learning disabilities. The costs to social programs, to taxpayers, and to the economy are staggering, to say nothing of the unquantifiable emotional, social, and financial costs to families of caring for a family member with a disability.

And yet, these children are not bad. They are not, by and large, unintelligent. They come from all family backgrounds, from all social strata, and from all races and religions.

But they are *frustrated*.

They are frustrated because they spend their formative years sitting in classrooms, unable to understand the lessons. They are frustrated because they know they can think, but they can't get information into their minds, and they can't get their thoughts and ideas out. They are frustrated because their peers, who are fundamentally no more brilliant than them, who are fundamentally no more capable than them, study and learn with some kind of ease while they struggle like Sisyphus with a stone too heavy for them to push.

That frustration has a profound effect on their psychological state. Their disability sets them apart from their peers, and time makes them dissociative. They drift further away. Although I believe firmly that we are all responsible for our actions and that we are all responsible for managing our own lives, I also recognize that the drugs, the alcohol, the violence, and the crime are far too often ways to escape a condition that these individuals were born with.

It is a condition that can be solved.

The hope for children who can't read, who can't learn, who can't succeed in school, is not empty. It is very real. It begins at the core of ability, at the beginning of the child's awareness of his world, in the sense that develops first. It begins with the right kind of activities that build the right foundation for learning and for life.

And beyond the solution to learning disabilities, I believe, there lies a greater hope. A great deal of the burden that these individuals place on society can be lifted. It can be lifted for a fraction of the cost that we incur every year we don't solve it.

Hope is an important ingredient in all of Mankind's great accomplishments. Perhaps more than anything, the faith that the impossible can be made possible has lifted our us from our primitive roots, has led explorers across continents and across oceans, has built great cities, civilizations, and cultures. Hope has allowed us to breach the most impregnable frontiers, from mountains to oceans to the limits of our own atmosphere. And as a child born in the Great Depression, I know without question that hope is there at the worst of times, like a ladder hung from heaven, enabling us to climb out even from the deepest holes.

But hope can also be an amorphous, unproductive thing. Without a pragmatic approach, without a plan of action and the determination to act upon it, instead of being our salvation, hope can become an obstacle in itself. The good feeling of possibility, unless it leads to action, becomes nothing more than a silver lining to the cloud of complacency.

And any lifetime is finite. By the time I had finally realized the role of the vestibular system and had begun to be able to describe with some clarity the science behind the profound effects of the Learning Breakthrough Program, I was well into my fifties and approaching the point in life when most people retire. I could see with glorious (and sometimes painful) acuity the tremendous benefit of balance-based therapies that exercise the underlying processes responsible for efficient neurological functioning, but there was still another obstacle to overcome. I did not have a clear plan of action that I believed would deliver these tools to the people who needed them.

Back in the 1960s, when I first saw that magnificent universe of forces operating around and within the children I was trying to teach, and when I first saw that it might be possible to use those forces to reach inside their brains and fix what was wrong there, I believed without a shred of hesitation that if I could actually do it, the society would enthusiastically embrace the significance of the ideas. Even through the frustrations of academia and the politics of the university, and even through struggles with neurologists, psychologists, and psychiatrists who were so convinced that learning disabilities were incurable that they could not open their minds to the possibility of a solution, and even while far too many children were overmedicated in an attempt to address the symptoms of a deeper and eminently solvable problem, I still believed that if the ideas were formulated and presented correctly, they would be embraced. Like Kevin Costner in his cornfield, I believed: "If you build it, they will come."

And they did. They came in twos and threes, in tens, in twenties. They came to the lectures I gave. They bought the Learning Breakthrough. They came—enough of them that we had food on the table and a roof over our heads, enough that Beverley and I could continue with our research. But I wanted to put a balance board under the feet of every child in the world. I wanted to hang a pendulum ball on a long string over every crib. I wanted there to be bean bags flying through the air in every classroom—and that goal takes a long time to reach by tens and twenties.

I continued to lecture. Many people scattered around the country can attest to the fact that I developed the habit of approaching new parents with their babies—in stores, restaurants, shopping centers, amusement parks, airports, and on city streets, ferries, and elevators—and telling them about the best tools they could make to organize their child's brain. I worked with teachers, therapists, and others around the world. It was immensely gratifying. But it was also slow going.

Then, in 2003, I met a man named Louis Weissman. Lou didn't have a background in developmental therapy. He was not a scientist. Or an educator. But from the first time we spoke, he brought the kind of energy, passion, and determination to our conversations that reminded me of the good friends who have always seemed to pop up at critical moments in my life. He had an unyielding commitment to helping people, which showed in everything he did. He had a no-nonsense sensibility that cut through obstacles toward its goal of getting the job done. And he was also a Harvard-educated businessman who, among many other accomplishments, had owned and run one of the most respected businesses in our nation's capital.

Like my other friends, he challenged me to make the Learning Breakthrough Program better, but unlike my other friends, his focus was not so much on the scientific rationale or on the program's effectiveness. He recognized that. But he was voraciously focused on making sure that people could understand and apply the program in their own living rooms easily and efficiently, and that they could consistently get results.

"What you have," he said, "is a set of materials that, when used correctly, gets results. And you have activities that people can do. But let's take a simple, programmatic approach. Let's create a series of daily activity sequences that will ensure that the materials are used correctly, that will teach people how to use them, and that will create immediate, observable results."

His argument made sense. Before I'd put the grid on the balance board, the children who had used it correctly had made significant gains, while the children whose feet were not lined up had achieved less. The grid established a structure that increased the user's results and made the program more effective. In the same way, a defined, daily program of activities would provide another form of structure and would make the program much easier to use.

It would also help to overcome the sometimes frustrating first phase of training. Some of the children I had worked with, the ones for whom performing physical tasks was so frustrating that they had wanted to give up, had been very difficult to keep on task. In some cases, warmth, nurturing, and motivation had not been enough. It had required discipline to get them past the threshold at which real progress and real results would begin to come rapidly. In a therapy environment or in a classroom, it was natural to maintain discipline, and it was natural to structure the program to keep the child on task, but I knew from experience that it was not always easy to achieve the same level of control at home. A program of daily activities would build that discipline into the home environment, and I knew that once the threshold had been reached, the child would naturally continue with the program to get better and better.

So Lou and I began to work together to convert a set of materials and a conceptual understanding of how to correct inefficiencies in brain processing into a structured program that we could be sure would create a real, observable improvement. While I refined and improved the activities, he worked with the presentation to make it polished, clear, and easy to use.

Years ago, I had made an activity video in my living room, but he suggested a new, professionally produced video that would lead people through the program, step by step. He also worked to simplify and to explain in greater detail the process of setting up the program to make it both more accessible and more intuitive. I had spent my life observing children and learning how to fix them; he had spent his life observing people and learning how to respond to their real, practical needs.

I had not imagined that "they would come" through a Web site operated by a passionate businessman, or that the Learning Breakthrough would become a "product" like toothpaste or superglue. But one of the great lessons Mr. Royer taught us was that if you can't solve a problem from one angle, come at it from another. That is how I had arrived at the realizations that led to the Learning Breakthrough Program, and as my friendship with Lou deepened and evolved into a partnership, I began to realize that a "product" was exactly what the program needed to be: a simple, easy-to-use, structured series of daily activities that would overcome the obstacles to learning, to action, and to operating at the highest level possible.

Lou also brought a new perspective to the work. The study that Jim Gage and Susan Workman had conducted with retirees in Alpine had played an important role in the development of my theoretical structure, but it had not shifted my myopic focus on applying the Learning Breakthrough Program to children with learning disabilities. With his business background, Lou's desire to help people is less specialized than mine, and he pointed out that there were other groups who could benefit—and, perhaps, who needed a program of this kind—just as much as learning-disabled children.

He talked, for example, of the need for rehabilitation for adults who had sustained brain trauma, particularly soldiers who return from combat with concussion trauma, ear damage from noise, or much more severe injuries. His experience in business had made him acutely aware of the intensely competitive nature of today's economy, and he pointed out that professionals, who today have less job security and more demanded of them than ever before, need every advantage they can get. And being a baby boomer himself, he brought special emphasis to the fact that his peers are now reaching retirement age in record numbers. Because of strained social systems, many will have to stay productive well into their retirement years, and because modern medicine is prolonging life, even those who are financially well off will have years after retirement for new adventures and experiences and will want their wits as sharp as possible. He proposed—and we began to create—refined programs for those groups, companions to the brain fitness software now available for older individuals, rehabilitation programs, and office-friendly therapies for the working world.

Ultimately, my focus will always be on children. There is a special energy that surrounds them, and I am most at home when I am with them, teaching them to live and learning from the immense force of life they carry with them. That day in my childhood when the pendulum's mysteries suddenly made sense, I saw an elegant orchestra of forces around it. Around a child, I see a symphony of possibility. Regardless of the child's age, background, abilities, or disabilities, to me that is the most beautiful symphony in the world. I cannot hear it without being compelled by its beauty or cringing when a sour note interrupts it. To the children I have known, I owe the greatest debt of gratitude: they have given me a life worth living. It is a debt I will never be able to repay.

But thanks to Lou and his business partner at Human Performance Group LLC Marc Stelzer, and to the invaluable partnership of business and thought that we have developed, the Learning Breakthrough Program will go wherever it is most needed. We will continue to refine it. We will continue to work to make it as effective as possible. We will continue to learn from the progression of discoveries that science will make, to understand better how the brain works—and how to make it work more efficiently.

We talk about the future like two college kids planning to change the world. Even though I am well into my seventies, and even though I need my own program on a daily basis to remain sharp, I don't think I've ever felt quite as young as I do now.

There are still more lions to find, more people to help, more balance boards to make, and more miles to travel.

Appendix:

THE SPACE WALK

Introduction to the Space Walk

Part of the purpose of this book is to provide some activities that can be done without any investment in materials, but which can have a positive impact on academic and work performance, intellectual clarity, and overall well-being. The Learning Breakthrough Program is an affordable, focused suite of activities and tools designed to directly impact the specific areas of the brain that underpin higher intellectual function. Its effects are more immediately recognizable and certainly more profound.

However, he Space Walk is something you can do today, on your own, without investing in materials and without the supervision of a professional therapist. One run through the series of activities will likely provide a clear picture of vestibular strengths and weaknesses, and repetition of the activities should, over time, promote the enhancement of your strengths and the improvement of your weaknesses. In turn, this will have a direct, positive impact on the physical workings of your brain.

Many activities make up the Space Walk, but they can be generally grouped under the headings of WALKING, HOPPING, RHYTHMIC HOPPING, and SKIPPING. I encourage parents to observe all of the activities in the space walk and see how they relate to each child's performance in the classroom. When you look for relationships between the space walk activities and academic performance do not just look at grades. Observe also how efficiently the child works to get the grades.

183

At the end of the book is a series of observations. It is a good idea to fill out an evaluation form for each child and to do these activities when you first start to use the Space Walk, and periodically thereafter. Certainly, the child who goes through the Space Walk activities each day, or several times a week, will improve at doing them, but almost certainly, his or her academic performance will improve also. Significant acceleration of the improvement can be obtained by using the Belgau Balance Platform activities in conjunction with the Space Walk.

WALKING ACTIVITIES

WALK

Walking is good exercise, a good observation activity and a necessary part of the Space Walk program. In an efficient walk, the posture is upright, the movement is steady and smooth, and the arms swing in a steady cross pattern (right arm moving with left leg and left arm moving with right leg). Often individuals with balance or integration problems will suppress one or both arms, will step farther with one leg or the other, or will have poor posture.

The human body and brain are, in a sense, a walking machine. This machine is designed to move through space as efficiently as possible. This walking machine is one big inverted pendulum made up of a series of other, lesser pendulums, all coordinated and integrated, oscillating through space. The arms and legs swing, counterbalancing one another. The hips and buttocks stabilize and counterbalance changes in the center of gravity that result from picking up a weight or shifting the arms out of the counter-balancing role to another role such as throwing an object or carrying a burden. The shoulders and trunk make up another pendulum. The dividing line between the top and bottom of the body is dynamic and changes as the need arises. The head sits on top another inverted pendulum, delicately balanced, maintaining a stable platform for the senses. Inside the skull, directly behind each ear in the vestibular organs, sits another pair of pendulums the called otolyth. All of these pendulums conspire to keep the head stable and steady, precisely referenced to the gravitational vertical so that the eyes and ears can orient and guide the body and brain in a dynamic and changing three-dimensional space.

184

A person with good vision can be walking and look at the 20/20 line on an eye chart and read the letters. The lines that make up the 20/20 letters on the Snellen Eye Chart are one minute of arc or one sixtieth of one degree wide at a distance of twenty feet. In order for the eye to resolve an image of that size from a distance of twenty feet, the eye must be held incredibly stable in space.

At the level of the feet and legs, there is movement and vibration in every direction. The hips and lower trunk smooth and dampen a great deal of this motion and vibration. The spine adds to the stabilizing influence of the lower trunk and hips. The spine especially dampens vibrations and motion along the vertical plane. The arms and shoulders counterbalance the leg motion and add their stabilizing effects. Together, the neck and the vestibular system refine the head stabilizing process, and the vestibular ocular reflex senses the motion that was not taken care of by the systems at all levels between the feet and head and moves the eyes to keep them perfectly centered on the target. Control is partially reflex, partially brain stem, reticular, and limbic, with the cortex connected and staying informed at all times. Information flows up and down the spinal chord, continuously commanding and monitoring the walking actions. If you reach up to scratch your ear or to slap a mosquito, the change in movement pattern is superimposed on the walking motion, the change in balance is computed, and a counterbalancing action is integrated into the overall activity. The same thing happens when you see an obstacle in your path and have to change the trajectory of the walk to step over it or walk around the obstacle.

If, while you are walking, you throw a ball or bean bag to your companion or just throw and catch the bean bag by yourself, the cortex calculates how you are going to execute and counterbalance the action and creates the proper motor program to carry it out. When the action is executed, the tactile, auditory, motor, and visual systems sense the action as it is being executed and, after it has been completed, the cortex integrates all the information that was generated from the time the action was conceived to its completion and evaluates it. If the results of the action do not accomplish what was originally intended, the cortex further analyzes the performance for glitches and updates the memory banks that support this kind of operation. The care and precision of the action and the final analysis depend on the emotional relativity of the action itself.

Over a lifetime, your walking patterns will have a profound impact on the quality of your life. The way you swing your arms when you walk has an impact on how your feet point. If your right foot is pronated (points inward as you walk), chances are that instead of your right arm swinging straight by your side, it is swinging out in the same direction that your foot is pointing. Perhaps you don't swing it as much as you swing your left arm. When you walk this way, your knee and hip are twisted inward and the joints in your foot, ankle, knee, and hip are not moving through the proper trajectories. If your left foot moves properly and straight, the right foot pointing inward not only affects your right leg and hip but also produces a slight twist in your pelvis and spine. You may get along and not have any great difficulty but you are more likely to have back, hip, knee, and foot problems, especially when you get older.

When you walk, you should stand straight; your head should be erect and level from side to side as well as from front to back. Your spine should be straight and your movement should be smooth, coordinated, and symmetrical. Your arms should swing smoothly, counterbalancing the motion of the legs. Your body should not appear rigid or floppy. You should not move with jerky, uncoordinated movements.

The foundation of a good walk is good balance. The foundation of good posture is good balance. It is profitable to observe children walking and to work to develop the child's ability to walk efficiently. Walking is, in itself, a good way to develop an efficient and coordinated walk. It is easier and, in most instances, faster and better to work on a great variety of balance activities along with working on the walk. Doing the activities that are included in the Learning Breakthrough Program along with the Space Walk activities are, by far, the best way to develop the brain processes that are important for achieving the greatest academic efficiency.

As both an introductory activity and again as a concluding activity to the space walk, the basic walk should be performed for a distance of about fifty feet. The child should be encouraged to maintain a steady pace and to swing the arms in a smooth, crosswise pattern, with the right arm moving to counterbalance the left foot and the left arm moving to counterbalance the right foot.

Specific things to look for are:
1. Is the posture erect?
2. Is the walk smooth, balanced, and rhythmic?
3. *Do the arms swing in a smooth, crosswise pattern?*
4. Is there any suppression of the arms?

Space Walk

The Space Walk Activities which develop a smooth walking pattern and the brain structures that support it are:
- toe on spot;
- walk heel to toe;
- sidestep, lead right;
- sidestep, lead left;
- march;
- march backwards;
- walk and turn clockwise;
- walk and turn counterclockwise;
- pick target, close eyes, and walk to target;
- close eyes, walk heel to toe on line; and
- zigzag walk.

TOE ON SPOT

A line about thirty to forty feet in length of randomly spaced spots slightly larger than a half dollar coin can be painted on the sidewalk or floor. The child is instructed to try to walk down the line of dots and place her toe on the dot so that the tip of the toe is perfectly centered on the spot. Precisely targeting the toe of each foot on a randomly spaced spot requires a higher level of balance and visual motor control than normal walking requires. This is a good activity for a child who has slow and labored handwriting, for a child who has trouble keeping her place in a book when she reads, for older children and adults who spend a lot of time sitting and working in front of a computer, and for people with neck or back problems. It gently stimulates the postural system. You can observe a child doing this activity and see how accurately she targets the toe and how balanced and relaxed she is while performing the activity. A teacher can watch how different children in the class do this activity and can learn to evaluate their performance. It is a good idea to observe *all* of the activities in the space walk and see how they relate to each child's performance in the classroom. When you look for relationships between the space walk activities and academic performance, do not just look at grades. Observe also how efficiently the child works to get the grades.

The faster this activity can be performed accurately, the higher the level of performance. Always strive for accurate and relaxed performance. The objective of the activity is to develop accuracy and precisely coordinated performance.

This activity, performed for a distance of thirty to forty feet, allows ample opportunity for the observer to assess the child's performance. Specific things to look for are:

1. Does the child target the spots precisely?
2. Does the child seem to overshoot or undershoot?
3. *Are the movements sloppy?*
4. Is the child demonstrating difficulty with balance?
5. Is the child unstable or uncomfortable?
6. Does the child contort his or her posture as the child moves down the row of dots?

WALK LINE HEEL TO TOE

The line should cover a distance of about twenty feet. Walking a line heel to toe requires the child to put one foot directly in front of the other foot, which increases the difficulty of maintaining balance. The child can walk down the line heel to toe forward, heel to toe backward, heel to toe with the eyes closed. He or she can walk the line sideways (leading with the right or left foot) or walk the line turning gently in a clockwise or counterclockwise direction. The line can be painted straight or it can be painted so that it curves or zigzags down the walk. If there is a lot of space available, three or four lines can be painted for children to walk.

This activity, performed for a distance of between twenty and thirty feet, allows ample opportunity for the observer to assess the child's performance. Specific things to look for are:

1. Was the child able to stay on the line?
2. Was the child able to place his or her feet precisely, with the heel to the toe when walking forward?
3. Was the child able to place his or her feet precisely, with the toe to the heel when walking backward?
4. Did the child able to maintain balance as he or she walks, or did the child become unbalanced?
5. Did the child appear stressed?
6. Are the arms relaxed or are they held in awkwardly to help maintain balance?

Sidestep, Lead Right

Sidestepping is a variation of the basic walk, but instead of facing forward on the line, the child's side of the body faces the line. For this exercise, the child's right shoulder should face the forward direction on the line. Instruct the child to smoothly sidestep, right foot first, along the line, and then move the left foot into position beside the right foot, taking the same size steps each time. It is important for the child to move smoothly and rhythmically.

This activity should be performed for a distance of about twenty feet.

Sidestep, Lead Left

This activity is similar to the previous one, except that, in this activity, the left side of the body faces forward on the line. Instruct the child to smoothly sidestep, left foot first, along the line, then move the right foot into position beside the left foot, taking the same size steps each time. It is important for the child to move smoothly and rhythmically.

This activity should be performed for a distance of about twenty feet.

MARCH

A march is a vigorous walk in which the feet are lifted higher than in a regular walk. Try to maintain the cross pattern swing of your arms and make your movements smooth and rhythmic.

This activity should be performed for a distance of about fifty feet.

MARCH BACKWARD

Marching backward is, of course, more difficult than marching forward. It is sometimes helpful to line up on a fixation point and then keep yourself on a straight course that way. Try to swing your arms in a cross pattern and lift your feet and knees high.

This activity should be performed for a distance of about twenty feet.

WALK AND TURN – CLOCKWISE

Walk and turn in a half clockwise circle as you move through the space. Keep swinging your arms in a cross pattern and try not to let the curve of your path disturb your smooth, rhythmic movements or the movement of your arms.

WALK AND TURN – COUNTERCLOCKWISE

This activity is the same as the previous one, except that your half circle turn will be in a counterclockwise direction.

PICK TARGET-- CLOSE EYES -- WALK TO TARGET

This activity should cover about fifteen feet of space. To lay it out paint "PICK A TARGET—CLOSE EYES—WALK TO TARGET " at the starting point. Paint four or five targets dots, labeled "A", "B", "C", "D", and "E" out on the course at different points. The targets should be strung out over the length of the allotted space, scattered randomly rather than lined up in a straight line, for this activity.

The child should pick one of the points, close her eyes, walk to the point that she has chosen, and put the tip of her toe on the point. When she thinks that her toe is touching the point, she should open her eyes to check and see how accurate she is.

Following are some variations to make the activity more challenging. Introduce these only after the child's performance has improved and she is becoming proficient at choosing a target and walking to it.

1. Ask the child to choose two targets. She can close her eyes, walk to the far target, turn around, and walk to the near target. Then she can open her eyes and check her performance.
2. Ask the child to select a target, close her eyes, and walk, turning clockwise or counterclockwise 360 degrees as she walks to the target.
3. Give the child a bean bag. Ask her to choose two targets, close her eyes, walk to the first target, stop, and throw the bean bag and hit the second target.
4. Give the child three bean bags. Ask her to choose a target to walk to and three targets to throw and hit with bean bags. Ask her to close her eyes and perform the sequence she has planned. She can walk to her target with her eyes closed, stop, and without opening her eyes, throw her bean bags at the targets. Then she can open her eyes and check her accuracy. This activity forces her to use her visual system at a higher level of performance than she would have to use to walk to a point and throw the bean bags at the three targets with her eyes open.

The vestibular sense is an inertial guidance sense as well as a balance sense. When the child closes her eyes and purposely moves through three-dimensional space to a goal, her primary guidance sense is the vestibular sense. When she looks out and picks a target to walk to, she mentally measures the space. If she closes her eyes and walks to the target, she has to internalize the space that she is going to walk through to reach her target. She must preplan the movement more precisely if she is going to do it with her eyes closed because she cannot see that she is deviating from her intended course and make slight corrections, as she can with her eyes open.

TWO FOOT HOP

The two-foot hop sequence should be performed in a space of approximately twenty to twenty-five feet.

The two-foot hop requires that the two sides of the body and the top and bottom halves of the body move together in a symmetrical, balanced, and coordinated manner to propel the body through space. When a child does the two-foot hop the two sides of the body should work in parallel. Watch and see that the two feet leave the ground and return to the ground at exactly the same time. Also observe the arms and top of the body and see if their thrust contributes to the hop or if their thrust works in opposition to the intended motion. Each hop should flow into the next hop and the body should move at the same rate through space. It should not be a hop-stop-then-hop-again movement sequence.

The first time a child performs the two-foot hop make sure that when she hops, she lands on the forward part of each foot. The toes need to hit the ground in order to absorb the landing shock before the heels hit. If the child jumps and her heels hit the ground first, she can injure her back seriously.. When the astronauts return from an extended stay in space they lose the timing control that is necessary to make the toes land before the heels. After a short period in the earth's gravitational field, their timing control returns. This clue tells the good detective that this activity has an impact on brain timing. The more efficient the hop, the more efficient is the brain timing. Performing this activity and related activities can be a factor in improving brain timing and coordination.

This activity, performed for a distance of between twenty and thirty feet, allows ample opportunity for the observer to assess the child's performance. Specific things to look for are:

1. Do the two sides of the body work in parallel?
2. Do the two feet leave the ground and return to the ground at exactly the same time?
3. Does the thrust of the arms and upper body contribute to the hop, or does it work in opposition?
4. Does each hop flow into the next hop, and does the body move smoothly through space?

HOP RIGHT

The hop right sequence should be performed in a space of about twenty feet from start to finish.

When a child hops on one foot her two arms and the top part of her body should move in parallel. Both arms should contribute positive thrust to the body's movement through space. She should hop in a straight line. Her hopping rhythm should be regular and not erratic. Poor rhythm, irregularly spaced hops, and a hopping pattern that does not go in a straight line, but rather weaves from side to side, are all indicative of a balance difficulty.

It is interesting to compare the efficiency level of the two-foot hop and the hop left, and the hop right sequences. A high percentage of right-handed children who have reading difficulties will hop more efficiently on the left foot than they do on the right foot.

To elaborate and increase the precision level of the hop activity, you can paint irregularly spaced target spots on the ground. The child can hop on the right foot and hit the target with the toe of the right foot when he or she hops.

This activity, performed for a distance of approximately twenty feet, allows ample opportunity for the observer to assess the child's performance. Specific things to look for are:
1. Does the child hop in a straight line?
2. Is the child's posture relaxed and upright?
3. Does the child have to lean to one side to stay balanced?
4. Are the hops regularly spaced?
5. Does the thrust of the arms and upper body contribute to the hop or does it work in opposition?
6. Does each hop flow into the next hop and does the body move smoothly through space?

HOP LEFT

The hop left activity is the same as the hop right activity, except that you hop on your left foot.

This activity, performed for a distance of approximately twenty feet, allows ample opportunity for the observer to assess the child's performance. Specific things to look for are:

1. Does the child hop in a straight line?
2. Is the child's posture relaxed and upright?
3. Does the child have to lean to one side to stay balanced?
4. Are the hops regularly spaced?
5. Does the thrust of the arms and upper body contribute to the hop or does it work in opposition?
6. Does each hop flow into the next hop and does the body move smoothly through space?

JUMP AND TURN

The jump and turn activity requires a space of about twenty to twenty-five feet.

Arrows can be painted in a line with each arrow pointing in a different direction. Zero degrees would point forward relative to the flow of the space walk. An arrow pointing 180 degrees would be pointing backward. An arrow pointing at 90 degrees would be an arrow pointing to the right and an arrow pointing 270 degrees would be an arrow pointing to the left. The child would look at the arrow, jump up in the air, turn, and land on the ground with his body facing in the direction the arrow is pointing. He would look at the next arrow and repeat the process. If he is at an arrow that is pointing forward and the next arrow is pointing backward or directly at him he would jump turn 180 degrees and land facing backward. If he looks at the next arrow and the arrow is pointing in the direction he is facing he has to jump up and turn 360 degrees. The controlled turning is a particularly valuable activity for developing and refining centering.

The utricle, a pendulum-like appendage in the vestibular apparatus, is the brain's primary sensor to orient the head to the gravitational vertical. There are two utricles. one on each side of the head buried in the bone, along with the three semicircular canals just behind each ear. When the head turns around its vertical axis, centrifugal force acts on the utricle on each side of the head and they swing out. If the head is perfectly aligned with the gravitational vertical, the utricles balance out because each utricle swings out an equal distance from the center line of the head and the gravitational vertical. If the center line or the rotation center of the head is tilted out of line with the gravitational vertical, one utricle moves farther out than the other. This provides an amplified out-of-vertical signal for the brain to deal with.

The brain is constantly recalibrating and maintaining its stability. The acceleration of gravity and the gravitational vertical are the brain's primary references for developing standards of measure for space, time, and energy. All of the brain's various processes are referenced to these standards. The more precisely the head is aligned with the gravitational vertical, the more precise the calibrating processes will be. The vestibular system, the eyes, and the neck work in a highly integrated manner. Controlled turns such as those in the jump and turn activity stimulate and refine this relationship.

Two different, but similar, versions of jump and turn can be incorporated into the space walk. The first version, described above and using right-angle arrows, identifies the direction in which the child should be facing when he or she lands. The child can turn (in mid-air) in whichever direction is easier for her to accomplish.

In the second version of jump and turn, the arrows are curved to indicate the direction in which the child must turn in mid-air (clockwise or counterclockwise). This version of the activity is much more difficult for the brain to organize and get accustomed to performing, but it is a very good exercise for strengthening the skills of space and directionality management.

HOP – TOES ON LINE

This advanced hopping activity requires more precision than jumping or hopping on only one foot with no particular landing target. In this activity, the child is instructed to land with her toes on the lines. The child may make several hops between the lines, and she may have to change feet as she hops, but the object is to arrive at the line, with the toes of the correct foot just touching the line.

Hop Right 2 – Left Two

This activity should cover a space of about twenty feet and requires the child to maintain a regular, rhythmic hopping pattern involving both balancing and sequencing. In this activity, the motion should flow smoothly from one side of the body to the other. The body should move forward at a uniform, constant rate and the top and bottom of the body should work in harmony. If the sequence is hop right, hop right, stop, reorient, hop left, hop left, stop, reorient, etc., there is inadequate bilateral integration. The child should do a variety of bilateral activities. Activities on the Belgau Balance Board also are valuable if a child has difficulty with this activity.

It is important to realize that this is a balance activity and a sequencing activity. To determine whether a child experiencing difficulty with this activity has a disability involving either balance or sequencing, reduce the balance level of the activity. Have the child sit down and watch as you tap on your knees, two taps on your right knee with your right hand, two taps on your left knee with your left hand. Ask the child to copy the sequence. Children whose eyes point to your right hand when you tap your right knee and to your left hand when you tap your left knee are generally able to copy the sequence, thus indicating a disability of the balancing skill. Children who stare straight at your hands and appear not to process the two right-two left pattern are unable to copy it.

This activity, performed for a distance of approximately twenty feet, allows ample opportunity for the observer to assess the child's performance. Specific things to look for are:
1. Does the motion flow smoothly from one side of the body to the other?
2. Does the body move forward at a uniform, constant rate?
3. Do the top and bottom halves of the body work in harmony?

Hop Left 2 – Right 1

This activity is a variation of the hop right two, hop left two activity above. Because fewer hops are involved, this activity requires a bit less space, only a space of about twenty feet.

Unlike the hop right two, hop left two activity, this activity requires the child to perform an irregular rhythmic sequence. The ability to carry out this kind of a sequence smoothly is basic to organizing and sequencing many academic processes. The higher the balance demands, the more difficult it is to perform this activity. Again, if a child has difficulty with this activity, it is easier to develop her ability to perform it if you reduce the balance demands. Sit across a small table from the child and have her watch your hands as you tap the right hand and the left hand to demonstrate the particular rhythmic pattern. After she has watched your hands as you do it a few times allow her to try to do just what you did. Once the child has successfully duplicated the sequence with her hands on the table, encourage her to try it again while hopping.

This activity, performed for a distance of approximately twenty feet, allows ample opportunity for the observer to assess the child's performance. Specific things to look for are:
1. Does the motion flow smoothly from one side of the body to the other?
2. Does the body move forward at a uniform, constant rate?
3. Do the top and bottom halves of the body work in harmony?

HOP Left 1 – Right 2

This activity is a variation of hop right two, hop left one, but the "feet" are switched. Like the basic activity on which this one based, this activity should cover a space of about twenty feet. The above explanation explains this activity also. By changing the balance emphasis from one foot to the other, this activity fosters comparable levels of balance between both sides of the body.

This activity, performed for a distance of approximately twenty feet, allows ample opportunity for the observer to assess the child's performance. Specific things to look for are:
1. Does the motion flow smoothly from one side of the body to the other?
2. Does the body move forward at a uniform, constant rate?
3. Do the top and bottom halves of the body work in harmony?

SKIP

Skipping is very like a "hop right two, hop left two" rhythmic hopping sequence through space. It requires good balance and good integration between the top and bottom of the body and between the two hemispheres of the brain. In an efficient, properly executed skip, the body is upright, the arms swing in a cross pattern, (right arm moving with left leg, and left arm moving with right leg), and the movement is smooth and rhythmic. Difficulties that are hard to observe in walking become more apparent in skipping because of the higher level of balance and more precise integration required. Faulty integration manifests itself in suppression of one or both arms, stiffness or rigidity of the trunk, uncontrolled or explosive movements of the arms, unstable or inconsistent rhythm, or abnormal shifting of the hips from side to side.

Gallop, Lead Right

Galloping is similar to skipping, except instead of a hop right two, hop left two rhythmic sequence through space, it involves a hop right two, hop left one rhythmic sequence. It is, essentially, a two short hops on the right foot and one longer hop on the left. Like the two-foot hop, the gallop requires good balance and good integration between the top and bottom halves of the body and between the two hemispheres of the brain. In an efficient, properly executed gallop, the body is upright, the arms swing in a cross pattern, (right arm moving with left leg, and left arm moving with right leg), and the movement is smooth and rhythmic.

The gallop, lead right activity should be performed for a distance of about twenty feet.

Gallop, Lead Left

This activity is similar to the previous activity, except that instead of leading with the right foot, the child leads with the left foot. The gallop, lead left activity should be performed for a distance of about twenty feet.

The Learning Breakthrough Program LEARNING BREAKTHROUGH PROGRAM has been updated for easy use in the home, school or clinic. Detailed information and ordering is available at www.learningbreakthrough.com or call 888-853-2762.

ABOUT THE AUTHOR

Eric Belgau is the youngest son of Frank and Beverley Belgau. After growing up in the Pacific Northwest and developing as an actor and playwright, he studied writing and drama at the University of Redlands, Johnston College. As a young adult, he wisely dropped acting and moved to Los Angeles to pursue a career in screenwriting.

In Los Angeles, his passion for writing and the purism he inherited from his father led him to independent filmmaking. His first original work was produced in 2004, followed by a second in 2006. In 2005 he began working in animation, writing pilot TV episodes for independent animation houses and has continued to work with independent animators around the world. In addition to his original work, he has rewritten seven independent features and a television miniseries, as well as selling and optioning projects to Hollywood studios.

Today, Eric lives in Burbank, CA, with his partner, Melissa Fertig, and their delightful daughter, Rhiannon. He is a founding member of the Wigigo Animation Collective and of Bay Film Studios in British Columbia, Canada, and when he isn't writing he advocates for renewable energy as a principal of an energy consulting and management group.

Dr. Frank Belgau
Creator of the Learning Breakthrough Program

For more information go to www.learningbreakthrough.com

CPSIA information can be obtained
at www.ICGtesting.com
Printed in the USA
LVHW060229230723
753132LV00015B/1335

9 781432 742072